Data Modeling with SAP BW/4HANA 2.0

Implementing Agile Data Models Using Modern Modeling Concepts

Konrad Załęski

Apress®

Data Modeling with SAP BW/4HANA 2.0: Implementing Agile Data Models Using Modern Modeling Concepts

Konrad Załęski
Warsaw, Poland

ISBN-13 (pbk): 978-1-4842-7088-2
https://doi.org/10.1007/978-1-4842-7089-9

ISBN-13 (electronic): 978-1-4842-7089-9

Managing Director, Apress Media LLC: Welmoed Spahr
Acquisitions Editor: Divya Modi
Development Editor: Matthew Moodie
Coordinating Editor: Divya Modi

Cover designed by eStudioCalamar

Cover image designed by Freepik (www.freepik.com)

Distributed to the book trade worldwide by Springer Science+Business Media New York, 1 New York Plaza, Suite 4600, New York, NY 10004-1562, USA. Phone 1-800-SPRINGER, fax (201) 348-4505, e-mail orders-ny@springer-sbm.com, or visit www.springeronline.com. Apress Media, LLC is a California LLC and the sole member (owner) is Springer Science + Business Media Finance Inc (SSBM Finance Inc). SSBM Finance Inc is a **Delaware** corporation.

For information on translations, please e-mail booktranslations@springernature.com; for reprint, paperback, or audio rights, please e-mail bookpermissions@springernature.com.

Apress titles may be purchased in bulk for academic, corporate, or promotional use. eBook versions and licenses are also available for most titles. For more information, reference our Print and eBook Bulk Sales web page at www.apress.com/bulk-sales.

Any source code or other supplementary material referenced by the author in this book is available to readers on GitHub via the book's product page, located at www.apress.com/978-1-4842-7088-2. For more detailed information, please visit www.apress.com/source-code.

Printed on acid-free paper

Table of Contents

About the Author

Konrad Załęski graduated from Warsaw University of Technology with a master's degree in management. After finishing his studies, he continued his education and completed two postgraduate courses in management information systems (Microsoft) and integrated information systems (SAP).

Konrad gained his experience by delivering business intelligence solutions for multiple global corporations. The majority of the projects from his portfolio were implemented on top of the SAP HANA, SAP BW/4HANA, and Microsoft BI platforms. He is also an active contributor and publisher in the SAP community.

About the Technical Reviewer

 **Attaphon Predaboon** is a certified SAP consultant and data and analytics manager at EY. He is passionate about finding innovative ways to use BI and analytics solutions to create business success.

He has led teams in business development, proof of concepts, and the deployment of SAP and many other data analytics technologies for various local and global firms.

About the Technical Reviewer

Introduction

This book is for anyone who wants to gain knowledge about the SAP BW/4HANA platform. In this book, readers will learn about new functionalities and components of SAP BW/4HANA and will get practical experience implementing agile data models using modern modeling concepts. This book is recommended especially for BI developers, consultants, and team leaders who have worked on previous versions of SAP BW, who are planning to upgrade their system to the SAP BW/4HANA release, or who have already started to explore SAP BW/4HANA and want to get a better understanding of what has changed and what the new options are.

This book contains the following chapters:

Chapter 1: SAP BW/4HANA Modeling Objects

This chapter gives a technical introduction to the SAP HANA and SAP BW/4HANA worlds. It walks readers through the main modeling objects, highlights new functionalities, and explains how to create these objects.

Chapter 2: Modeling Concepts

This chapter introduces five modeling concepts, highlighting their usage as well as the pros and cons of each. The next chapters will use these modeling concepts to implement solutions that meet the requirements of the given business scenarios.

Chapter 3: Publishing HANA Objects Through BW/4HANA

This chapter will explain how to expose HANA objects through the BW/4HANA layer without creating a persistent acquisition layer. In addition, readers will learn how to pass input parameters between BW queries and HANA calculation views.

Chapter 4: Creating a Field-Based Data Model

This chapter presents how to create field-based data models on top of HANA objects. After this chapter, readers will know how to implement star schema models without using InfoObjects.

Chapter 5: Creating a Hybrid Data Model

This chapter explains the hybrid modeling approach used to mix a field-based approach with SAP InfoObjects. With this approach, you will be able to enhance your model with additional information even though it is not available in the source objects.

Chapter 6: Integrating SAP and Non-SAP Data into a Single Data Model

This chapter demonstrates how to combine SAP and non-SAP data to create a single integrated data model that provides a 360-degree view on the data.

To understand each aspect of the modern modeling concepts, I recommend starting with Chapter 1 and reading through the book sequentially.

CHAPTER 1

SAP BW/4HANA Modeling Objects

This chapter gives an overview of the main modeling objects that are available in a SAP BW/4HANA application. I will walk you through the modeling objects from both the SAP HANA and SAP BW/4HANA worlds. In this chapter, you will learn how the existing modeling objects have changed and what the new modeling artifacts are.

Modern Data Modeling

SAP BW/4HANA was introduced in 2016 as a next-generation business warehouse to replace the old SAP BW application. The core design interface for the BW modeling tools has been now unified. This means that the SAP GUI is no longer required for modeling activities. BW/4HANA offers a completely new modeling platform, which brings numerous benefits to developers.

- Simplified modeling, with four modeling objects instead of nine

- Focus on and significant extension of the virtualization capabilities

© Konrad Załęski 2021
K. Załęski, *Data Modeling with SAP BW/4HANA 2.0*,
https://doi.org/10.1007/978-1-4842-7089-9_1

- Modern, easy-to-use, Eclipse-based modeling
  environment

- A unified UI for the BW/4HANA modeling tools (the
  SAP GUI is not used for modeling anymore, and the
  SAP BEx Query Designer has been replaced with an
  Eclipse-based Query Designer)

- A single environment for BW and HANA modeling

From a functional perspective, in addition to all the new features and
functionalities, one of the biggest advantages of BW/4HANA is the ability
to use hybrid modeling. Developers can now combine modeling artifacts
from both the SAP BW and SAP HANA worlds.

The big modeling difference between SAP BW and BW/4HANA is that
the latter enables agile data warehousing capabilities, which were missing
in previous versions of this product. The big change in BW/4HANA
modeling is that it enables a field-based modeling approach, which saves
a lot of development time and effort, especially when creating proof of
concepts or pilot data models. Although InfoObject-based modeling
still is the core of enterprise datawarehouses (EDWs), in some scenarios
there is no point in creating dozens of InfoObjects to simply deliver a
prototype. Also, often a business needs an ad hoc report to perform
analysis on a specific set of data. For example, a business may require a
report that will be used for only one specific project or a one-time activity
(like a data extract). In such a scenario, there is no point in enhancing an
existing enterprise data model, which is usually a huge effort, because
the developer needs to perform a fit-gap analysis, check the impact on
the existing model, consider the risk factors, and finally implement the
solution based on the design. With BW/4HANA, it is possible to create
ad hoc reports independently from an EDW without even persisting the
data, just by taking advantage of HANA's in-memory processing features
to implement the logic that will process and display the results on the fly
based on the source tables.

The big step forward within BW/4HANA is a virtualization capability. This concept utilizes a feature of HANA virtual tables that can be later consumed by BW/4HANA modeling objects. Virtual modeling allows you to avoid data persistency when accessing data from other databases. With virtualization, it is possible to integrate non-SAP data within SAP data models or even create independent data models based on external data sources. Of course, when creating virtual data models, we need to consider performance constraints. Since the data will be sourced from external systems, we will not be able to get any benefits from the HANA in-memory processing powers. Unlike standard BW data models, where complex joins and expressions are precalculated and stored physically, in the virtual approach all the operations will be processed on the fly whenever a user runs a report.

Main SAP HANA Modeling Objects

As mentioned, within BW/4HANA it is possible to take advantage of the SAP HANA native modeling artifacts.

Two main modeling objects in SAP HANA are calculation views and table functions. Calculation views are modeled using the graphical interface of the SAP HANA modeler perspective, and hence no deep SQL knowledge is required. Table functions are created with the SAP HANA development perspective and are purely based on SQL scripts.

Graphical calculation views (CVs) are modeled using the SAP HANA modeler perspective. They are used to model a business logic and return a desired set of data as output. With CVs you can perform data manipulation functions such as joins, unions, aggregations, and ranks, as well as apply filters and create calculated columns. A node-by-node building approach enables an easy way of implementing and maintaining complex business logic.

In the past, there were three kind of CVs: attribute views, analytic views, and calculation views. Within SPS11 this approach has been unified, and all three view types were replaced with a single modeling object called a *calculation view*. SAP also provided functionality for migrating analytic and attribute views to calculation views. Although all these view types are still available in Eclipse, the ones that are deprecated should not be used anymore.

Table functions (TFs) are SQL-based modeling objects that are used whenever the functionality of a graphical CV is not sufficient to meet the business requirements. The usage of TFs is similar to CVs, but the main difference is that the entire logic is developed by using SQL scripts instead of the graphical editor. Also, the Eclipse perspective used for TF development is different. Unlike CVs, TFs are created using the SAP development perspective of the Eclipse tool.

TFs are used to implement the business logic, however, from a reporting perspective, they cannot be used as stand-alone objects. Once a table function is created, it needs to be exposed through the calculation view created on top before making it available on the reporting layer.

Table functions were introduced as a replacement to SQL script calculation views. Using the Eclipse migration tool, developers can automatically convert obsolete script-based calculation views into table functions.

As you can see, the main purpose for modeling both objects is to perform complex data manipulations on top of tables or other views. In the next sections, I will describe how to create these objects and explain the use cases, advantages, and limitations of each of them.

Calculation View

To start working with calculation views, go to the SAP HANA modeler perspective, right-click the package, and select New ➤ Calculation View (Figure 1-1).

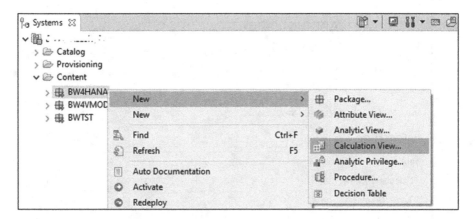

Figure 1-1. *Creating a new CV*

After selecting the Calculation View option, the window for defining the general settings of the CV will open (see Figure 1-2).

In Figure 1-2, these two fields are important:

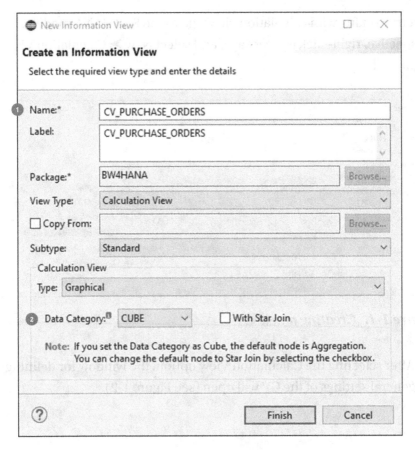

Figure 1-2. *New Information View window*

1. *Name*: This is a mandatory field that is the technical
   name of the calculation view.

2. *Data Category*: This field has the following options:

   a. *CUBE*: The last default node in the graphical editor
      will be Aggregation. Views of this type can be
      consumed by reporting tools. At least one output
      column needs to be specified as a measure.

    b. *DIMENSION*: The last default node in the graphical editor will be Projection. Views of this type cannot be consumed by reporting tools. All the output fields are attributes (measures are not available).

Note   Once the calculation view is created, you will be able to change the data category type at any time without rebuilding the entire view logic.

After providing the calculation view details, the next step is to model the business logic in a graphical designer. Calculation views are built using building blocks called *nodes*. Graphical views support the following node types:

- *Join*: Join operations are used to link two data sources based on specific columns. When linking the data sets, you can choose the type of join (referential, inner, left outer, right outer, full outer, or text join) and can indicate the join cardinality (1..1, 1..n, n..1, n..m).

- *Union*: These operations are used to combine two or more data sources. SAP HANA is a columnar database, so wherever possible, it is always better to use union nodes than joins.

- *Projection*: This is the node that retrieves data from the target source objects. It allows you to select fields, apply filters, or create calculations. The Projection node can consume the following source objects: table, virtual table, view, calculation view, table function, or any other node within the model.

- *Aggregation*: This allows you to aggregate data based on selected attributes and apply basic aggregation functions (Sum, Min, Max, Count, Avg, Var, StdDev) on selected measures.

- *Rank*: Within this node, it is possible to filter the data based on the rank definition. In addition, this node allows you to automatically generate rank columns.

The most commonly used node is Projection, which simply reads the data from the underlying table. Nodes are being added to the model by dragging and dropping them from the palette (see Figure 1-3).

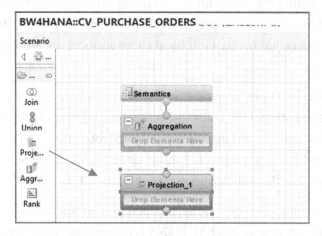

Figure 1-3. *Adding a Projection node to the calculation view*

Adding all the other node types is the same. Once we have the node added to the model, in the next step we need to define the source table (or any other object like other calculation view, table function, or database view). By clicking the Add Objects button, you can search for the desired view or table.

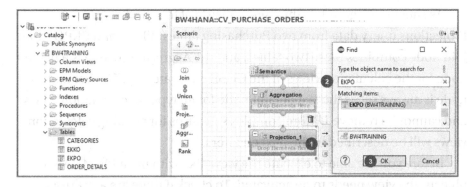

Figure 1-4. *Adding an object to the Projection node in a calculation view*

When searching for the object, you should type its name (Figure 1-4). Once it is found and displayed in the "Matching items" section, select it and click OK to proceed. Another way to add source objects is to drag them from the left display pane directly onto the node (the "Drop Elements Here" section displayed on the node). Figure 1-5 shows an exemplary calculation view that joins two standard ERP tables for Purchasing Document Header (EKKO) and Purchasing Document Item (EKPO) on the Document Number column (EBELN).

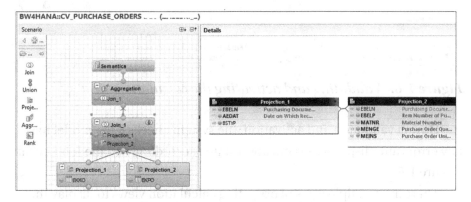

Figure 1-5. *Calculation view for puchase orders*

As shown in Figure 1-5, this view consists of four nodes: two
Projections query data from two Purchasing tables (EKKO and EKPO), the
Join node combines these two tables, and the Aggregation node is a default
node for the calculation views of the CUBE data category. The Semantics
node is always set as the last default node for all types of calculation views
and cannot be removed. More complex scenarios for creating calculation
views will be described in the next chapters.

Before you are able to execute the view, like with most BW/4HANA
objects, the view needs to be activated. To check if there are any errors,
you can first validate the view by clicking the Validate button. Once it's
validated, you can activate it, as shown in Figure 1-6.

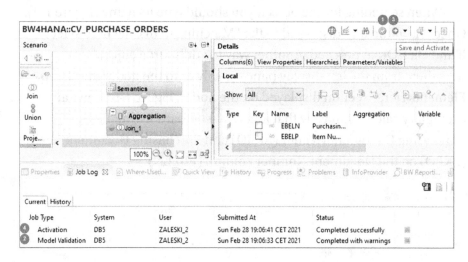

Figure 1-6. *Validating and activating the calculation view*

During validation and activation, the system checks if the model has
any errors and displays the activation status accordingly on the Job Log tab
(Figure 1-6).

There are multiple ways of executing calculation views to display the
results. The first option is to right-click the Semantics node and select the
Data Preview option. The system will then open a new tab (Figure 1-7),

where you can see the output of your view on the Raw Data tab (by default 200 records are displayed).

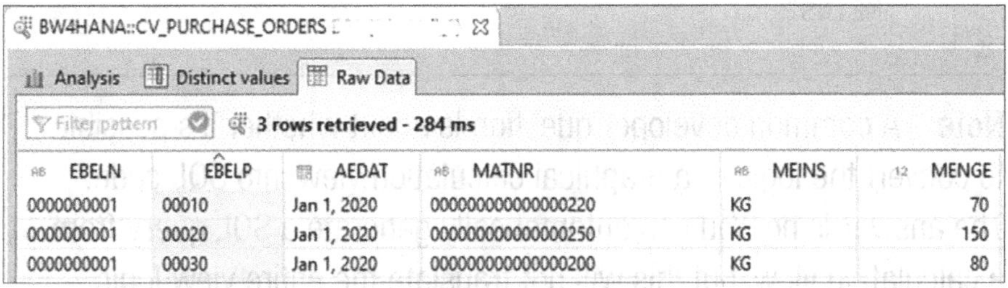

AB EBELN	EBELP	AEDAT	AB MATNR	AB MEINS	12 MENGE
0000000001	00010	Jan 1, 2020	00000000000000220	KG	70
0000000001	00020	Jan 1, 2020	00000000000000250	KG	150
0000000001	00030	Jan 1, 2020	00000000000000200	KG	80

BW4HANA::CV_PURCHASE_ORDERS ⌗

Analysis | Distinct values | Raw Data

Filter pattern ✓ ⌗ 3 rows retrieved - 284 ms

Figure 1-7. *Data preview of calculation view*

The second option is to right-click the calculation view's name in the package tree in the left pane (on the System tab). There you have two options to run the view: Data Preview and Generate Select SQL. The Data Preview option works the same way as Preview on the Semantics node (see Figure 1-7).

The Generate Select SQL option opens the SQL console and generates the SQL SELECT statement on top of the calculation view. This option is useful when you want to perform ad hoc analysis combining the output of the view with additional source objects like other calculation views or tables. When using this option for the calculation view CV_PURCHASE_ORDERS, the following SQL code is generated:

```
SELECT
        "EBELN",
        "EBELP",
        "AEDAT",
        "MATNR",
        "MEINS",
        sum("MENGE") AS "MENGE"
FROM "_SYS_BIC"."BW4HANA/CV_PURCHASE_ORDERS"
GROUP BY "EBELN",
```

```
"EBELP",
"AEDAT",
"MATNR",
"MEINS"
```

Note   A common developer question is about whether it's possible to convert the logic of a graphical calculation view into SQL code. The answer is no. You can automatically generate a SQL query from a calculation view, but this will not translate the entire view logic into SQL joins and unions; instead, this will simply create a SELECT statement on top of that calculation view.

While starting work with calculation views, you might face some issues even though the view logic was modeled properly. Here are the most common problems that you might encounter:

Issue: In the SQL console, the developer can query the data from specific schema tables, but when trying to activate a view on top of one of these tables, there is the following error message:

Create Scenario failed: The following errors occurred: user is not authorized (2950)

Reason: Runtime objects are created by the system user _SYS_REPO, who needs to have the SELECT privilege to the schema.

Solution: Grant the SELECT privilege for that schema to the _SYS_REPO user. You can assign the privilege by running the following SQL code:

```
GRANT SELECT ON SCHEMA "SCHEMA_NAME" TO _SYS_REPO WITH GRANT
OPTION
```

Figure 1-8 shows the SQL console with the code for granting the SELECT privilege to the _SYS_REPO user for the schema called TEST_SCHEMA.

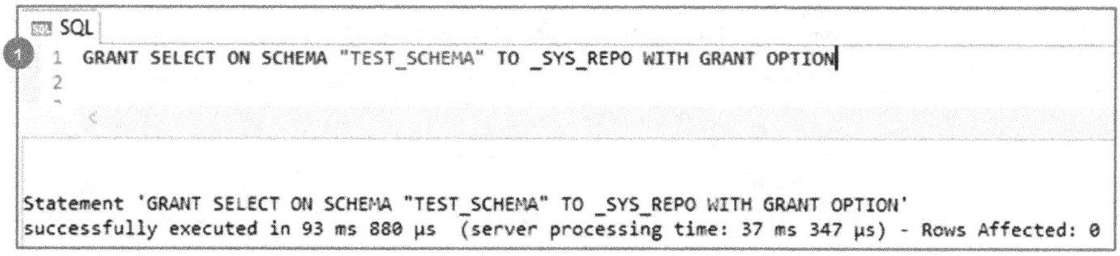

```
SQL
1  GRANT SELECT ON SCHEMA "TEST_SCHEMA" TO _SYS_REPO WITH GRANT OPTION
2
```

```
Statement 'GRANT SELECT ON SCHEMA "TEST_SCHEMA" TO _SYS_REPO WITH GRANT OPTION'
successfully executed in 93 ms 880 µs  (server processing time: 37 ms 347 µs) - Rows Affected: 0
```

Figure 1-8. *Granting a privilege to the _SYS_REPO user*

Issue: In the SQL console, developers are able to query the data from specific schema tables, but when trying to perform a data preview on a calculation view, there is the following error message:

Error: SAP DBTech JDBC: [258]: insufficient privilege

Reason: SQL analytic privileges have been applied for the calculation view.

Solution: In the semantics of the calculation view, go to the View Properties tab and apply the option Classical Analytic Privileges instead of SQL Analytic Privileges (see Figure 1-9). Another method is to assign the calculation view to the Analytic Privilege object assigned to the user or user role.

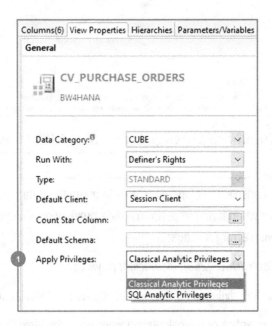

***Figure 1-9.** Applying privileges in a calculation view*

Issue: When executing a data preview on each calculation view node, no data is returned in the output, despite that data in the underlying tables exists.

Reason: In the calculation view properties, Session Client is set as a default client.

Solution: In the semantics of the calculation view, go to the View Properties tab and change the Default Client value from Session Client to Cross Client (see Figure 1-10).

Figure 1-10. *Setting the default client in the calculation view*

Calculation views are the main modeling objects in the SAP HANA environment. Thanks to the graphical interface, developers can easily incorporate most of the business logic into data models without deep SQL programming knowledge. Calculation views provide a lot of development flexibility, so the maintenance is also not a big challenge. In some scenarios, however, the functionality available in calculation views may not be sufficient. Here are the common limitations of SAP HANA calculation views:

- There is no way to implement loop functions (WHILE <condition> DO, etc.) using a graphical view.

- Window functions (LAG, LEAD, DENSE_RANK, etc.) are not available.

- Complex SQL functions (STRING_AGG, WORKDAYS_BETWEEN, etc.) are not available.

- Application function libraries are not supported.

Fortunately, there is a second modeling object called a *table function*, which supports more complex scenarios, but it requires SQL programing knowledge.

Table Functions

Let's now create a table function with the same logic as the calculation view created in the previous section. As presented in Figure 1-5, a calculation view was created as a join of tables for Purchasing Document Header (EKKO) and Purchasing Document Item (EKPO). A join was performed on the Document Number column (EBELN).

Personally when I start working on table function logic, I prefer to build the entire code in the SQL console. Once I run the code and validate the results, I copy the SQL script to a TF object and apply the required adjustments. With this approach, it's easier to debug the code if there are any issues and also preview the results of that code. Here you can find the SQL code for joining the EKKO and EKPO tables:

```
SELECT EKPO."EBELN", EKPO."EBELP", EKKO."AEDAT",
EKPO."MATNR",  EKPO."MEINS", EKPO."MENGE"
FROM "TEST_SCHEMA"."EKKO" EKKO
JOIN "TEST_SCHEMA"."EKPO" EKPO ON EKKO."EBELN" = EKPO."EBELN";
```

Figure 1-11 shows the SQL console with the results of executing the previous code.

⊞ SQL 📄 Result					

```
⊖ SELECT
        EKPO."EBELN", EKPO."EBELP", EKKO."AEDAT", EKPO."MATNR", EKPO."MEINS", EKPO."MENGE"
   FROM
        "TEST_SCHEMA"."EKKO" EKKO
        JOIN "TEST_SCHEMA"."EKPO" EKPO ON EKKO."EBELN" = EKPO."EBELN"
```

	EBELN	EBELP	AEDAT	MATNR	MEINS	MENGE
1	0000000001	00010	Jan 1, 2020	00000000000000220	KG	70
2	0000000001	00020	Jan 1, 2020	00000000000000250	KG	150
3	0000000001	00030	Jan 1, 2020	00000000000000200	KG	80

Figure 1-11. *SQL script to link the EKPO and EKKO tables*

After executing the script provided in Figure 1-11, you can see that the
results are the same as the output of the calculation view created in the
previous section. As a next step, I will switch the Eclipse perspective from
the SAP HANA modeler to the SAP HANA development perspective. If this
perspective has not been used before, the first step is to create a repository
workspace from the Repositories tab, as in Figure 1-12.

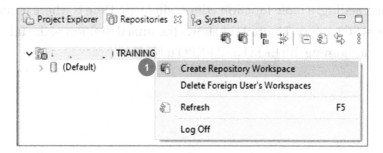

Figure 1-12. *Create Repository Workspace menu item*

After providing the name and physical path for the workspace, it is
ready to use. Within the tree under the created workspace, I will search for
the package where I want to create a table function. To open the wizard,
right-click the specific package and select New ➤ Other. A selection wizard

will pop up. Input **Table Function** to find the right object, as shown in Figure 1-13.

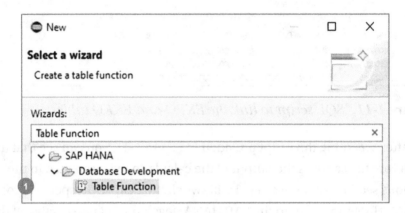

Figure 1-13. *Creating a table function wizard*

Once Table Function is selected, provide a name for the table function. After proceeding, a table function editor will open. Here is where to paste the actual SQL query. Figure 1-14 shows the final definition of the table function for joining the EKKO and EKPO tables.

```
Table Function          ①
  1  FUNCTION "_SYS_BIC"."BW4HANA::TF_PURCHASE_ORDERS" ( )
  2
  3  ②  RETURNS TABLE
  4      (
  5          "EBELN" VARCHAR(10),
  6          "EBELP" VARCHAR(5),
  7  ③      "AEDAT" DATE,
  8          "MATNR" VARCHAR(18),
  9          "MEINS" VARCHAR(2),
 10          "MENGE" INT
 11      )
 12
 13      LANGUAGE SQLSCRIPT
 14      SQL SECURITY INVOKER
 15  ④  DEFAULT SCHEMA "TEST_SCHEMA"
 16      AS
 17
 18  BEGIN
 19
 20  ⑤  RETURN
 21
 22      SELECT
 23          EKPO."EBELN", EKPO."EBELP", EKKO."AEDAT", EKPO."MATNR", EKPO."MEINS", EKPO."MENGE"
 24  ⑥  FROM
 25          "EKKO" EKKO
 26          JOIN "EKPO" EKPO ON EKKO."EBELN" = EKPO."EBELN"
 27      ;
 28
 29  END
```

Figure 1-14. *Definition of table function to link the EKPO and EKKO tables*

In Figure 1-14, I highlighted the important part of codes, which should always be defined explicitly by the developer.

1. By default when creating a new table function, the editor uses your local schema. Consider changing this value to the schema that is accessible to other users. In my opinion, the most appropriate schema is _SYS_BIC, which is also where all the column views generated by calculation views are stored.

   FUNCTION "_SYS_BIC"."BW4HANA::TF_PURCHASE_ORDERS" ( )

2. The table value should be set to the TF output type.

   RETURNS TABLE

19

3. In this section, you need to list all the columns
    returned in the actual SQL code. You need to
    preserve the column order and column names
    (which are case sensitive). Also, make sure that the
    data types are consistent with all the data types of
    the source columns returned in the query.

```
(
"EBELN" VARCHAR(10),
"EBELP" VARCHAR(5),
"AEDAT" DATE,
"MATNR" VARCHAR(18),
"MEINS" VARCHAR(2),
"MENGE" INT
)
```

4. This section is optional; however, if you are utilizing
    tables within the schema, which is named differently
    in a production environment (i.e., on a development
    environment the schema is named TEST_SCHEMA,
    but on a production system, the same schema is
    named as PROD_SCHEMA) you should always
    provide this parameter in TF definition. If you
    provide the default schema in the definition of a
    table function, then during the transport to the next
    environment, this schema will be automatically
    replaced with the schema of the target system (based
    on the schema mapping definition).

```
DEFAULT SCHEMA "TEST_SCHEMA"
```

5. Add the RETURN phrase before the final SELECT statement.

```
RETURN
```

6. Add your actual SQL SELECT query followed by a semicolon (;). If you use in the table function definition the DEFAULT SCHEMA parameter, then you should remove all the schema names from the query (use "EKKO" instead of "TEST_SCHEMA"."EKKO")

```
SELECT EKPO."EBELN", EKPO."EBELP", EKKO."AEDAT",
EKPO."MATNR", EKPO."MEINS", EKPO."MENGE"
FROM "EKKO" EKKO
JOIN "EKPO" EKPO ON EKKO."EBELN" = EKPO."EBELN"
```

To test the table function, go to the SQL console and write a SELECT statement, providing the full name of the TF in the FROM clause.

```
SELECT * FROM "_SYS_BIC"."BW4HANA::TF_PURCHASE_ORDERS" ( ) ;
```

Figure 1-15 shows the results of the SQL statement, which queries the data from the table function.

	SQL	Result
	SELECT * FROM "_SYS_BIC"."BW4HANA::TF_PURCHASE_ORDERS" ( )						

	EBELN	EBELP	AEDAT	MATNR	MEINS	MENGE
1	0000000001	00010	Jan 1, 2020	00000000000000220	KG	70
2	0000000001	00020	Jan 1, 2020	00000000000000250	KG	150
3	0000000001	00030	Jan 1, 2020	00000000000000200	KG	80

Figure 1-15. *Querying the table function for purchase orders*

After creating and activating the table function, to make its output available for reporting, I need to create a calculation view, which will use a TF as a source. Although this calculation view is created on top of the table function, its properties will be the same as for a regular calculation view (use Figure 1-2 as a reference). The only difference is that the view will consist of a single Projection node, pointing to the table function object as a source. Figure 1-16 shows a calculation view that queries data from a table function.

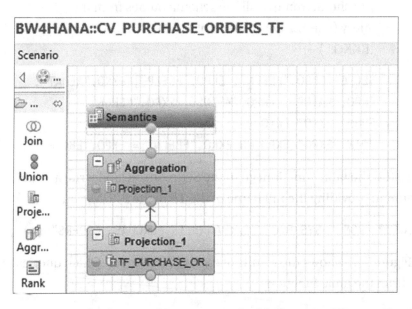

Figure 1-16. *Calculation view on top of table function for purchase orders*

One of the disadvantages of using table functions is that they are error-prone. Here I listed common activation issues when working with table functions:

Issue: When activating a table function, there is the following encoding error shown:

Unsupported encoding Cp1250 for the '<table function name>' file; only UTF-8 encoding is supported.

Reason: The default file encoding is set in the Eclipse tool as Cp1250.

Solution: From the Eclipse toolbar, select Window ➤ Preferences ➤ General ➤ Workspace and set UTF-8 as the text file encoding value (see Figure 1-17).

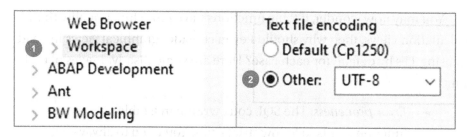

Figure 1-17. *Eclipse text file encoding*

Issue: When activating a table function, there is a mismatch error:

Could not create catalog object: return type mismatch;

Reason: Columns listed in a TF definition do not match the columns listed in the final SELECT query.

Solution: Make sure that the list and order of columns in the specified final SELECT query matches the list and order of columns listed in the TF definition. Always explicitly define the column names and avoid using an asterisk (SELECT * FROM...) to select all columns from a table.

Issue: When activating a table function, there is a syntax error:

Syntax error in table function object: incorrect syntax near "END"

Reason: A semicolon is missing after the SELECT statement.

Solution: Add a semicolon after the last SELECT statement. Each block of code within the TF definition should be followed by a semicolon (;).

Issue: When activating a table function, there is a general error:

Could not create catalog object: general error; RETURN statement should be defined for table function

Reason: The RETURN phrase is missing in the TF definition.

Solution: Add the RETURN phrase before the final SELECT statement.

You may now wonder, if table functions have more functionality than calculation views, then why should I even consider graphical views instead of using TFs by default for each case? Here are some disadvantages of table functions:

- *Error proneness*: The SQL code written in a table function needs to follow strict rules. You need to always remember to preserve the column order, explicitly provide the proper data types, and use semicolons after each block of code.

- *Maintenance*: It is much more difficult to implement enhancements to a complex SQL query than to graphical views.

- *SQL knowledge*: A developer needs to know SQL well to be able to implement complex and well-performing queries.

- There are limitations for passing multivalue optional input parameters.

Despite all these disadvantages, I prefer using table functions over calculation views. This is mainly because in my projects, there were scenarios where complex calculation views needed to be enhanced with functions, which are not supported by the graphical designer. For these cases I needed to either rebuild the entire logic as SQL code or create a table function on top of an existing calculation view to apply additional functions, which were not achievable in the graphical view. Anyway, wherever possible, I suggest sticking to the graphical approach because of the maintenance.

Virtual Tables

With the functionality of Smart Data Access (SDA), HANA offers the ability to bring in data from external systems without having to replicate it in the SAP HANA database. With SDA, developers can easily establish remote connections, which allows you to create virtual tables and access these objects as if they were local HANA tables.

In the BW/4HANA landscape, SDA can play an important role when it comes to creating non-SAP data models or integrating external data into SAP data models. Having data from multiple systems (like Oracle, SQL Server, Hadoop, and others) integrated into a single SAP enterprise data warehouse enables new analytics capabilities.

Another benefit of SDA is that it is a cost- and time-efficient solution. First, you don't need to replicate the data and pay for the storage. Of course, for large data sets and complex models, there still might be a need to persist external data in the BW/4HANA layer due to performance reasons. Second, there is no need to set and maintain the replication system. Moreover, data accessible via SDA is real-time. Thanks to virtual tables, you can create queries consuming external data and combine them with data residing in the SAP HANA system.

To start accessing remote data sources, you need to first set up the connection. The easiest way is to create a new remote source using the Eclipse GUI (as an alternative for creating a remote source, you can also use a SQL script). To establish the remote connection, open the SAP HANA modeler perspective and expand the Provisioning catalog. Then right-click the Remote Sources folder and select New Remote Source, as shown in Figure 1-18.

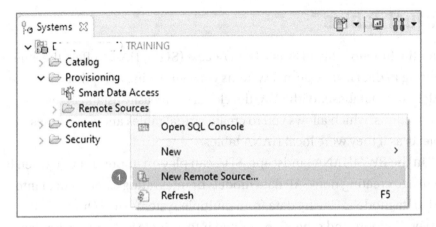

Figure 1-18. *Creating a remote source (SDA)*

After providing all the connection properties, the remote source object will be available under the Remote Source catalog. Each remote source will contain the database name and a list of all accessible schemas and tables (see Figure 1-19).

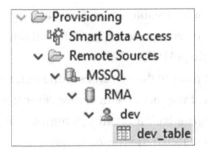

Figure 1-19. *Remote data sources view*

As shown in Figure 1-19, there is a remote connection, named MSSQL, to a database called RMA. This RMA database contains a schema called dev, and within that schema there is a table named dev_table. At this point you will not be able to query data from that table yet.

To start querying data from remote source tables, you need to create a type of HANA object called a *virtual table* first. Virtual tables need to be created for each remote table that you want to later access.

Tip Before creating virtual tables, a good practice is to create a SAP HANA database schema that will be dedicated to remote tables. This way all the virtual tables will reside in one place.

Like with remote sources, there are two ways to create virtual tables: using a GUI or using a SQL script. Figure 1-20 presents a graphical way of creating a virtual table.

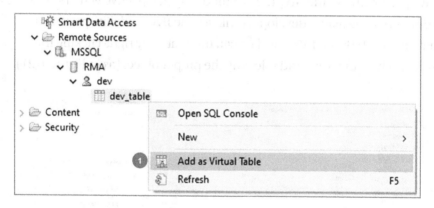

Figure 1-20. *Creating a virtual table*

Note   For each remote source, you need to have authorization to create virtual tables. The following SQL query grants this privilege:
GRANT CREATE VIRTUAL TABLE ON REMOTE SOURCE
<SOURCE_NAME> TO <USER_NAME>

After selecting the option for adding a virtual table, as a next step you need to enter the name of the virtual table and the target schema. Once this information is provided and confirmed, the virtual table will be created under the given schema. You can start using the virtual table in the SQL console or consume it in graphical views if it is a regular HANA table.

Main SAP BW/4HANA Modeling Objects

Within the BW/4HANA SAP unified user interface for all modeling objects, developers can now develop all the BW objects using the Eclipse tool (see Figure 1-21). An additional benefit is that they can switch from the HANA native perspective to the BW/4HANA modeling perspective with a single click. To develop BW artifacts, developers will use the BW modeling perspective of Eclipse. Each BW/4HANA artifact can be created by right-clicking the InfoArea, choosing New, and selecting the proper object (as in Figure 1-21).

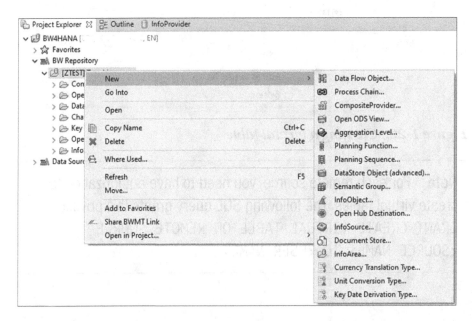

Figure 1-21. *Modeling objects in the BW modeling perspective*

For specific BW/4HANA tasks, there is still a need to use the SAP GUI. To unify its usage with modeling activities, the SAP GUI has also been embedded in Eclipse. By clicking the Open SAP GUI button (or using the keyboard shortcut Ctrl+6), you can open the SAP GUI within the Eclipse tool (see Figure 1-22).

Figure 1-22. *SAP GUI in Eclipse*

SAP BW/4HANA simplifies the data modeling approach by limiting the number of modeling object types from nine to just four. For data persistency, there are no more objects called InfoCube, PSA, DSO, or HybridProvider. They all have been replaced with a single object called Advanced DSO (ADSO). When it comes to the virtual layer, the following legacy objects were merged into a single object called CompositeProvider: MultiProvider, InfoSet, and VirtualProvider. There is also one new modeling object called Open ODS View available. The object Open ODS View has functionality similar to the former VirtualProvider object. The main purpose and functionalities of InfoObject remain the same. Figure 1-23 shows how BW/4HANA simplified the modeling objects in comparison to the old SAP BW system.

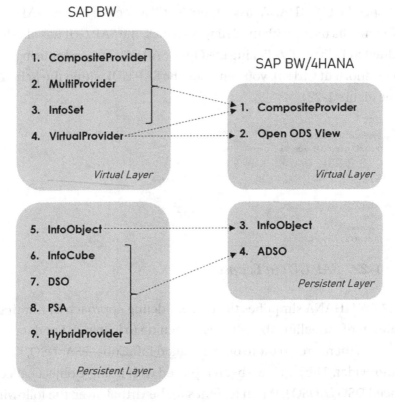

Figure 1-23. *Comparison of modeling objects within BW versus BW/4HANA*

The most elementary modeling artifact is InfoObject. The main functionality of this object has not changed with the BW/4HANA release. Developers who were working on previous versions of SAP BW will be familiar with this object. In the next section, I will not focus on the details of the InfoObject properties; I will highlight the functionalities that can be useful in the new modeling approach.

Open ODS Views are objects representing a virtual modeling layer. This means they do not persist any data. With Open ODS views, developers can bring external data into the BW reporting layer. Unlike InfoObjects, with Open ODS Views you can decide what the elementary building block is. They can be built based on InfoObjects, another Open ODS views, or raw fields.

With Open ODS View objects, developers can easily manage external data sources and build star schema models without data persistency. This means they can act as a kind of virtual master data or virtual fact table. In addition, with the Open ODS View object's field-based approach, we avoid creating too many InfoObjects, which in some scenarios (proof of concepts, pilots, tables/views data provisioning) does not bring any value, but generates additional work for creating multiple dummy objects in the system.

In SAP BW/4HANA, the functionalities of objects like DSO, InfoCube, PSA, and HybridProvider have now been unified into a single modeling object. The primary object of BW/4HANA for data persistency is the ADSO. Unlike the old BW persistent objects, ADSOs do not need to be based solely on InfoObjects; they can be implemented using a field-based modeling approach. There are business scenarios for creating ad hoc reports, proof of concepts, or models on external sources that need to be loaded into the BW/4HANA system. While defining the ADSO structure, you can simply list all the required fields and data types and activate the object. You also don't need to specify what building block type you will use for ADSO; you have the flexibility to mix InfoObjects with raw fields within a single ADSO.

CompositeProvider is a BW/4HANA object that combines all the functionalities of former MultiProviders, InfoSets, and VirtualProviders in one. CompositeProvider represents a logical layer, so it does not persist any data (virtual object). It enables you to merge data coming from multiple InfoProviders or HANA calculation views before creating the final query used for reporting. A good BW/4HANA modeling practice is to use CompositeProvider as a logical layer, which is later consumed by the final Query object. CompositeProviders support two main operations: join and union. In addition, with the latest release of BW/4HANA 2.0, it is possible to combine multiple join and union operations within a single CompositeProvider. Thanks to that, building logical models is similar to building calculation views. Node types available for modeling composite providers are also almost the same as for calculation views. You can implement complex scenarios combining InfoProviders and calculation views using join, union, projection, and aggregation nodes.

BW/4HANA 2.0 additionally empowers CompositeProvider with HANA SQL script capabilities. Therefore, CompositeProvider offers the ability to implement SQL-based calculated columns. This is a nice improvement, since the functionality of creating calculated columns on characteristics was always missing in the old BW system. With this feature, you can easily create calculated columns that will, for example, concatenate values from two InfoObjects into a single string. All the SQL calculations will be processed on the fly during the query execution, meaning that for complex calculations and large data sets performance can be impacted. SQL scripts can be also leveraged for implementing filter expressions on InfoProviders consumed in the CompositeProvider model.

To summarize, here are the main benefits and enhancements of CompositeProvider within BW/4HANA 2.0:

- CompositeProvider can combine multiple PartProviders (ADSOs, Open ODS Views, InfoObjects) into a single logical layer.

- SAP HANA calculation views are supported as PartProviders.

- The output structure of CompositeProvider can be built using a mix of InfoObjects, Open ODS Views, and raw fields.

- Projection, aggregation, join, and union modeling nodes are available.

- Join operations give more flexibility with the option for selecting the join type (inner, referential, left outer, right outer, full outer), setting join cardinality (n.m, 1.n, n.1, 1.1), and using the join operator (=, ≠, <, ≤, ≥, >).

- SQL scripts are supported for implementing filter expressions and calculated columns.

Query objects are used for reporting and can be consumed by front-end tools. They can be created on top of each InfoProvider, but in my opinion it is always better to create a CompositeProvider as an intermediate layer between an InfoProvider and a final Query object. This provides more flexibility in case you want to apply some additional logic to the underlying InfoProvider or combine it with other InfoProviders. In such a scenario, you will not be forced to re-create a query from scratch, but just enhance the logical layer and continue using the current query. In SAP BW/4HANA, the BEx Query Designer tool is not supported anymore. A feature of the BEx designer has now been migrated to the Eclipse platform. In other words, the functionality of the BEx Query Designer is now available as an Eclipse-based Query Designer.

In this chapter, I will not walk through all the functionalities of queries, since most of them are the same as in the SAP BEx Query Designer. This chapter is focused on the data modeling capabilities; hence, I will only give a high-level overview of the Query Designer.

A new object available in the BW/4HANA system that might be useful for modeling is a Data Flow object. Data Flow objects graphically explain dependencies between selected BW/4HANA objects. Thanks to Data Flow objects, you can create a template for your data flow and generate all the objects from the graphical model.

In the next sections, I will present a high-level overview of BW/4HANA objects, trying to highlight features that in my perspective are useful in the new modeling approaches.

InfoObject

When creating a new InfoObject using an Eclipse BW modeling
perspective, on the General tab you will find two check boxes for
generating external SAP HANA views. By default they are grayed out, but
once you select Master Data and Usable as InfoProvider options, they will
become active (see Figure 1-24).

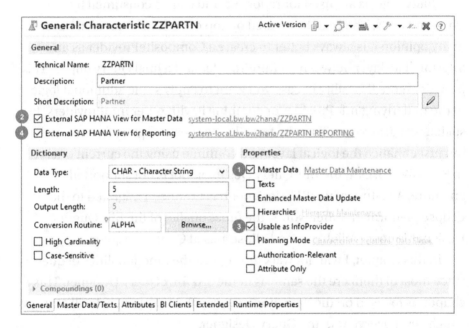

Figure 1-24. *InfoObject external SAP HANA view options*

As shown in Figure 1-24, the Master Data check box activates the
External SAP HANA View for Master Data option, and the Usable as
InfoProvider check box activates the option External SAP HANA View for
Reporting. After activating the view, you will see the location of each HANA
view that was generated from the InfoObject.

Note   The default location for generating views out of BW objects is system-local.bw.bw2hana. However, you can define a different location using the transaction RS2HANA_VIEW.

When I switch to the SAP HANA modeler perspective and navigate to the package path shown in Figure 1-24, I will see two created HANA views, which were generated after InfoObject activation. The first calculation view is named the same as the InfoObject. The name of the second one is a combination of the InfoObject and a trailing _REPORTING string (see Figure 1-25 as a reference).

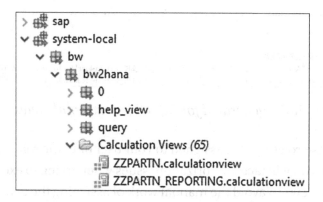

Figure 1-25. *Calculation views generated from the InfoObject*

In addition to the naming, the main difference between these two views is that the view generated for the Master Data object (ZZPARTN) is of the DIMENSION data category type, which means it cannot be consumed by reporting tools and all the output fields are the Attribute type. ZZPARTN_REPORTING is a CUBE-type calculation view, which can be used for reporting and consists of both attributes and measures. Depending on your needs, you can decide which type of external view is more suitable in your scenario.

Note   There are multiple restrictions for generating external HANA views from BW objects, so you should not select that option for every single InfoObject by default. For more information about restrictions for generating SAP HANA views from the BW/4HANA system, refer to the official SAP documentation.

External HANA views are generated with the SQL Analytic privilege. During the generation of external HANA views, for each view there is also a new role generated. Figure 1-26 displays two roles that were generated for two external views for the ZZPARTN InfoObject.

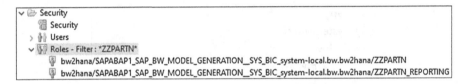

Figure 1-26. *Roles generated for InfoObject external views*

Until these roles are not assigned to your user or to the role assigned to your user, you will face authorization issues when trying to execute the external view. To avoid the manual work of assigning the generated role to the user every time a new external view is created, it is possible to automatically assign these roles to the user/role for each external view (tcodes: RS2HANA_ADMIN, RS2HANA_CHECK).

External views generated from BW/4HANA objects should not be manually modified. This is because the external view will be regenerated every time the InfoObject is activated, so all the manual changes will be overwritten with the default settings. If you want to perform any additional data manipulation for that object, you need to create a regular calculation view that will use the external view as a source. In the next chapters of the book, I will walk through some use cases where I will make use of InfoObject external views.

Another InfoObject functionality that I find as useful is the SAP HANA View option set as the Read Access Type parameter. This feature can be utilized while creating virtual data models. Once the SAP HANA View access type is set, you do not need to load any data into the InfoObject structures; instead, simply indicate the SAP HANA view as a source and apply the associations between the calculation view fields and the InfoObject attributes (see Figure 1-27).

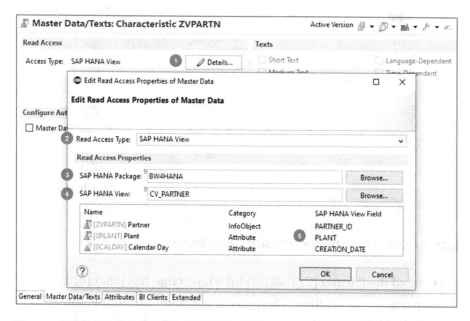

Figure 1-27. *InfoObject with SAP HANA View access type property*

As shown in Figure 1-27, the InfoObject ZVPARTN has the SAP HANA View access type set. It reads data from the calculation view CV_PARTNER, which resides in the BW/4HANA package. The InfoObject ZVPARTN is mapped to the PARTNER_ID field of the calculation view. The InfoObject attributes 0PLANT and 0CALDAY are mapped to the view fields PLANT and CREATION_DATE accordingly.

The last feature of the BW/4HANA InfoObject that from my perspective is worth noting is the transitive attributes feature. I will introduce this functionality based on the example presented in Figure 1-28.

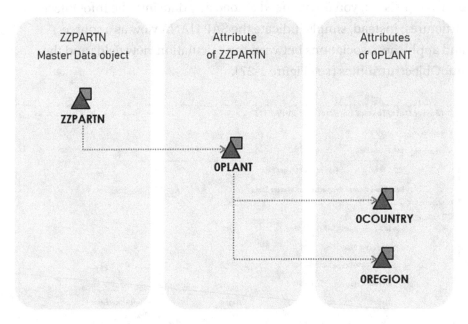

Figure 1-28. *Use case for transitive attributes*

I created the Partner (ZZPARTN) InfoObject that has Plant (0PLANT) set as a navigational attribute. Despite the information about Plant associated with Partner, the reporting requirement is to also display the Country (0COUNTRY) and Region (0REGION) values of that Plant attribute. These two fields are navigational attributes of Plant. To fulfill this requirement, I want to make both the Plant and Plant attributes available as navigational attributes of the Partner (ZZPARTN) InfoObject. This requirement can be met by maintaining transitive attributes for the ZZPARTN InfoObject. On the Attributes tab, right-click the Navigation Attributes pane and select "Maintain transitive attributes" (Figure 1-29).

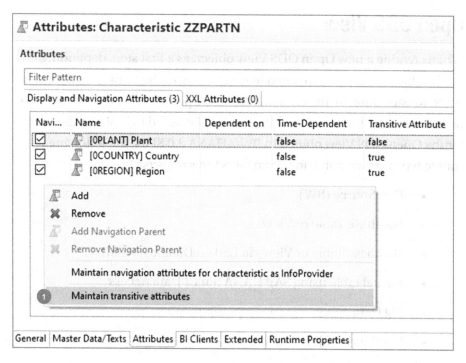

Figure 1-29. *"Maintain transitive attributes" option for InfoObject*

Once you select Transitive Attributes from the maintenance window, the attributes will appear in the Display and Navigation Attributes section. In this section, there is a Transitive Attribute column, and based on that, you can identify whether a specific field is a regular attribute or transitive. As shown in Figure 1-29, the attributes 0COUNTRY and 0REGION have been marked with the flag true in the Transitive Attribute column. With this configuration, the Country and Region columns can be used for the reporting, although they will not be physically loaded into the Partner (ZZPARTN) master data table. Transitive attributes simplify development, reduce the maintenance, and eliminate redundancy.

Open ODS View

When creating a new Open ODS View object, as a first step, depending on the object's purpose, we need to choose one of the semantics options: Facts, Master Data, or Texts. As mentioned, Open ODS View objects do not persist any data, so as a second step we will be asked to indicate the source for the Open ODS View object. In BW/4HANA 2.0 SP04, the following source types are available for Open ODS View objects:

- DataSource (BW)

- Database Table or View

- Database Table or View via Linked Database or MDC

- Virtual table using SAP HANA Smart Data Access

- Big Data

- DataStore Object (Advanced)

- Transformation

After selecting the source object for the Open ODS View object, we can start defining its structure based on the source fields. Figure 1-30 presents the General tab of the modeling editor for the Open ODS View object.

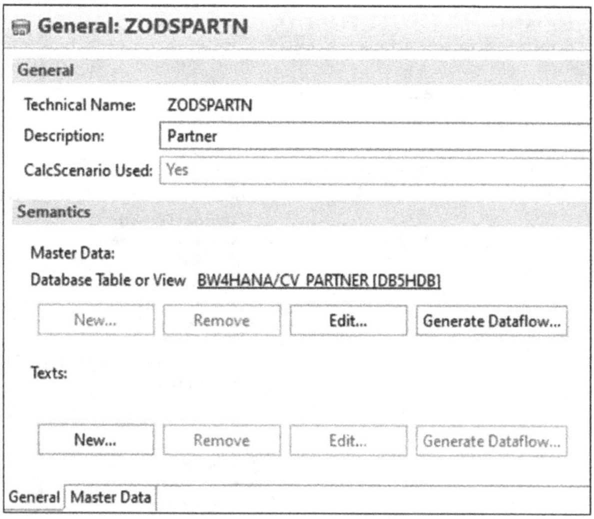

```
🖥 General: ZODSPARTN

General

  Technical Name:      ZODSPARTN
  Description:         Partner
  CalcScenario Used:   Yes

Semantics

  Master Data:
  Database Table or View  BW4HANA/CV_PARTNER [DB5HDB]

      [   New...   ]  [  Remove  ]  [   Edit...   ]  [ Generate Dataflow... ]

  Texts:

      [   New...   ]  [  Remove  ]  [   Edit...   ]  [ Generate Dataflow... ]

General  Master Data
```

Figure 1-30. *Open ODS View editor: General tab*

The General tab is available always, no matter the semantics type
chosen when creating an Open ODS View object. For the given example
(Figure 1-30), Open ODS View objects use as a source the CV_PARTNER
calculation view. The Edit option allows you to change the source object.
The Generate Dataflow option gives you the ability to automatically
generate the data source and ADSO (with transformation and DTP)
between the source object and the Open ODS View object. This option can
be useful in the future if we want to improve the performance by persisting
the underlying data in ADSO, without changing the Open ODS View
structure. In the next chapters of the book, I will describe this functionality
in more detail with an example.

The second tab of the Open ODS View editor may differ depending on
the chosen semantics type. In the given example, I selected Master Data
as the semantic type; hence, the second tab is named Master Data (see
Figure 1-31).

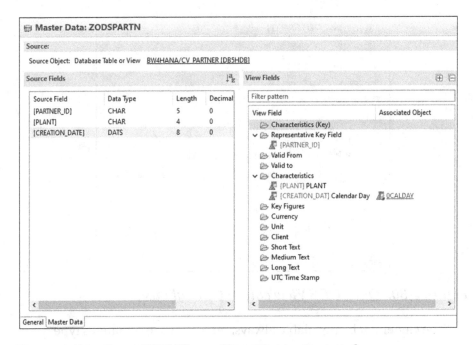

Figure 1-31. *Open ODS View editor, Master Data tab*

Within this tab I will model the structure of the Open ODS View object. In the left pane, there is a section called Source Fields, where you can find a list of all fields available in the source object. To select the source fields, which should be used to model the Open ODS View object, you can simply drag and drop them from the Source Fields section to the View Field section. For the Open ODS View objects of Master Data type, it is mandatory to indicate one field that should be placed under the Representative Key Field group. In my example, I set the PARTNER_ID field as the representative key field. The two remaining fields: PLANT and CREATION_DATE have been assigned to the Characteristic section. As you could also notice, PARTNER_ID and PLANT are raw fields, which were taken directly from the source, whereas the CREATION_DATE field has been associated with the 0CALDAY InfoObject.

In this exercise, I created the Open ODS View ZODSPARTN, which has functionality similar to the InfoObject ZVPARTN created in the previous section of that book. The main difference is that to build the Open ODS view, I didn't have to use any single InfoObject (I used 0CALDAY for field association just to demonstrate the functionality). Thanks to that, creating Open ODS View objects is extremely flexible and fast. This object is especially useful when you need to manage external data models for which master data has not been created in the BW/4HANA landscape yet. This can save a lot of development time, which would be consumed for creating dozens of InfoObjects for each dimension field when using the old BW system.

Advanced DSO

Advanced DSO consists of three technical tables: inbound, active, and change log. In addition to technical tables, there are also three database views generated (these are not calculation views): a view for extraction, a view for reporting, and a view for external access. Database objects generated for ADSO are stored in the SAPABAP1 schema. Table 1-1 presents the naming patterns for the database-generated ADSO objects.

Table 1-1. *Database Objects Generated for ADSO*

Object Type	Object Name	Description
Table	/BIC/A<ADSO name>1	Inbound table
Table	/BIC/A<ADSO name>2	Active data table
Table	/BIC/A<ADSO name>3	Change log
View	/BIC/A<ADSO name>6	View for extraction
View	/BIC/A<ADSO name>7	View for reporting
View	/BIC/A<ADSO name>8	View for external access

The behavior of each technical table can differ depending on the ADSO settings. In general, the inbound table acts as a new data table and stores the data load details. The active table contains data that is utilized for reporting purposes. The change log table keeps track of all the data changes within the ADSO. External SQL HANA views might be used when implementing routines with ABAP or AMDP/SQL scripts in BW/4HANA transformations.

The ADSO editor consists of three tabs: General, Details, and Settings. Figure 1-32 presents the General tab of the ADSO editor.

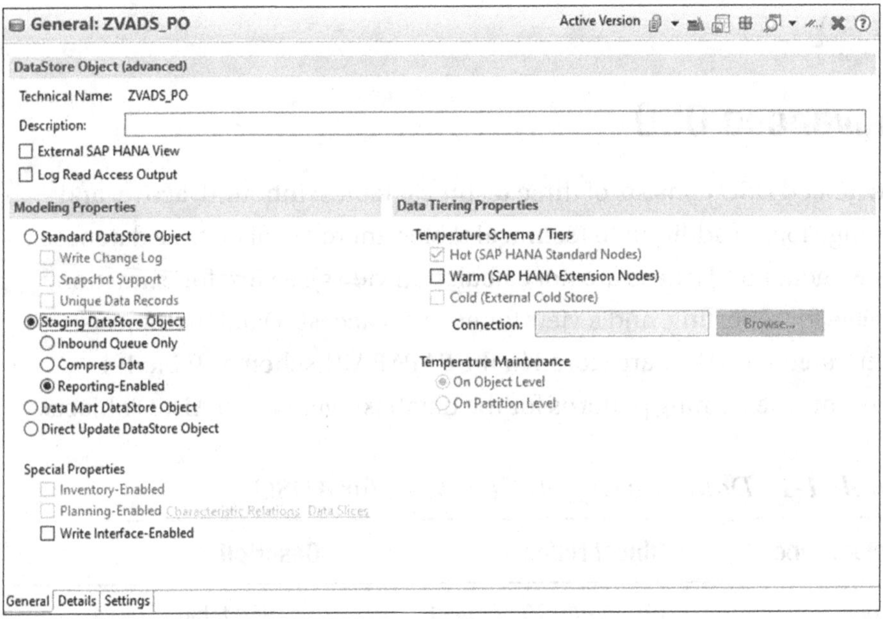

Figure 1-32. *Advanced DSO editor: General tab*

On the left pane of the General tab, you can configure the modeling properties of an ADSO. As shown in Figure 1-32, there are the following modeling properties for an ADSO:

- *Standard DataStore Object*: This type can cover most reporting scenarios. Within this type there are additional settings available.

    - *Write Change Log*: Once this option is selected, when loading the data, the delta will be saved in the change log table. The change log stores the request activation history; hence, when this option is selected, it is possible to roll back data from the state before request activation.

    - *Snapshot Support*: This option is active only if the Write Change Log check box is selected. This option is useful when the ADSO is loaded always with a full load. Data that is not available in the load request is being removed from the active table of the ADSO and written to the change log table.

    - *Unique Data Records*: This option should be selected if the ADSO will be loaded always with unique records. This speeds up the ADSO request activation process. The request activation will fail if the data set will contain a field combination that already exists in ADSO.

- *Staging DataStore Object*: For this type, the change log is not supported. The following properties are available:

    - *Inbound Queue Only*: This type of ADSO can be used for the staging layer and cannot be used for reporting. All data is stored in a single inbound table.

45

- *Compress Data*: Data is initially written to
  the inbound table. During activation they are
  compressed (aggregated based on semantic key)
  and loaded to the active table. During activation,
  key figures are either summed up or overwritten
  (depending on aggregation type defined on the
  transformation level). Since the change log table is
  not used, it is not possible to perform requests by
  request deletion.

- *Reporting-Enabled*: This property is similar to the
  Compress Data option, with the difference that
  during request activation, data from the inbound
  table is not removed. In the reporting scenarios,
  data is taken from the active table; however, for data
  extraction the inbound table will be queried.

- *Data Mart DataStore Object*: The behavior of this ADSO
  type is the same as the functionality of the former BW
  object called InfoCube. This type should be used when
  loading additive deltas (key figure values cannot be
  overwritten; only MAX, MIN, and SUM aggregations are
  allowed). Data is initially loaded to the inbound table.
  During activation it is compressed and loaded to the
  active table. For this type of ADSO, all fields are treated
  as keys. When using this type of ADSO in reporting,
  data is fetched from the union of inbound and active
  tables, meaning that even if the load request is not
  activated, the report will return all the data.

- *Direct Update DataStore Object*: When using this type, data is loaded to the active table directly. No other technical tables are used. Request activation is not possible, and data for extraction and reporting is fetched always from the active table. Data can be written using DTP or an API.

In addition to the modeling properties, on the General tab of the ADSO editor (Figure 1-32) there is also a Data Tiering Properties section. Using this property, you can implement a data tiering storage strategy depending on the data category (Hot, Warm, or Cold).

The second tab available while creating an ADSO is the Details tab. On this tab, the actual ADSO modeling is taking place. Figure 1-33 shows the Details tab of ADSO called ZVADS_PO.

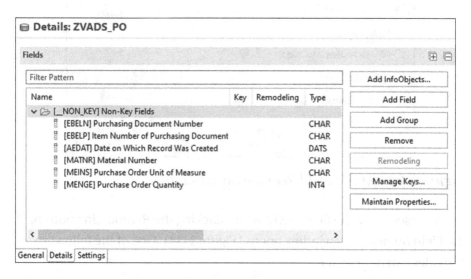

Figure 1-33. *Advanced DSO editor, Details tab*

When creating a new ADSO, you can provide an object (DataSource, InfoProvider, InfoObject, or InfoSource) as a template. Thanks to that, all the InfoObjects/fields will be derived to the ADSO structure from the template object. Of course, it will be possible to change/remove some of them according to the needs. In the example shown in Figure 1-33, when creating the ADSO, I used DataSource as a template. All the fields available in the selected DataSource has been generated in the Fields section. You might notice that ZVADS_PO consists of raw fields. By clicking Add InfoObject or Add Field, you can add a new entry to the Fields section. The Add Group button allows you to add a new folder to the ADSO field structure. With the Remove button, you can remove the selected fields. The Remodeling button enables the options shown in Figure 1-34.

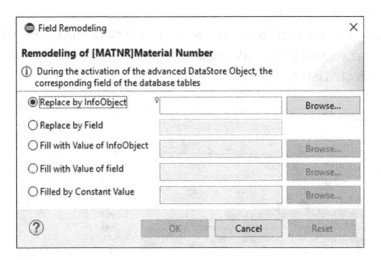

Figure 1-34. *ADSO Field Remodeling window*

After selecting the field MATNR and clicking the Remodeling button, the Field Remodeling window opens (Figure 1-34). One of the following activities can be selected:

- *Replace by InfoObject*: The specific field/InfoObject will be replaced with a different InfoObject.

- *Replace by Field*: This specific field/InfoObject will be replaced with the raw field. The given name should not already be in use for the ADSO.

- *Fill with Value of InfoObject*: This will load values from the given InfoObject into the remodeled field/InfoObject.

- *Fill with Value of field*: This will load values from the given field into the remodeled field/InfoObject.

- *Filled by Constant Value*: This will load constant value into the remodeled field/InfoObject (only new elements can be filled).

In Figure 1-33, there are two remaining buttons: Manage Keys and Maintain Properties. Depending on the ADSO configuration, the Manage Keys button can be either inactive or mandatory. It is used to indicate a key fields/InfoObjects combination that uniquely identifies each record.

With the Maintain Properties button, we can set the properties of the field/InfoObject (aggregation type or behavior of the master data check). You can find more field properties in the right pane of the Details section (the pane will appear once you click a specific field/InfoObject).

CompositeProvider

When creating a new CompositeProvider, like for all other objects, as a first step we need to provide its technical name. Optionally we can enter the description and name of another CompositeProvider from which we want to copy the structure. On the next screen, we are able to select the source PartProviders and default operation (a join or union). We can also skip this step by clicking Finish and going to the CompositeProvider editor directly. The system by default opens the General tab of the editor, as shown in Figure 1-35.

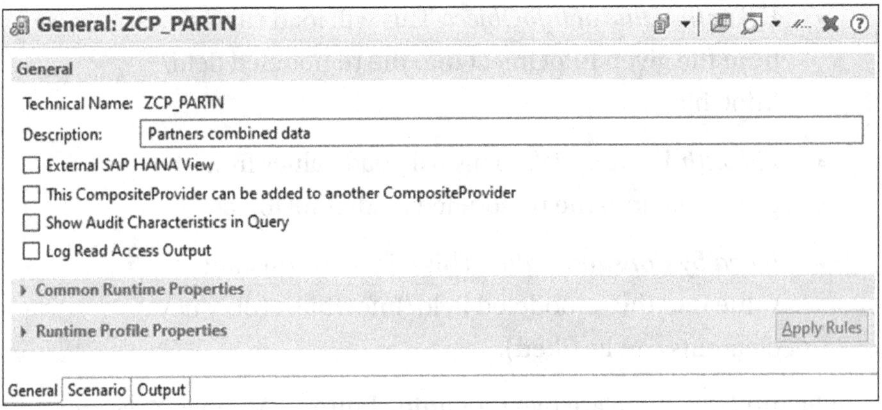

Figure 1-35. CompositeProvider, General tab

On this tab, you can configure the runtime properties of the CompositeProvider. Here you can also find a check box for generating an external SAP HANA view from the CompositeProvider. You can also specify whether this CompositeProvider can be consumed as a provider by another CompositeProvider (option "This CompositeProvider can be added to another CompositeProvider").

The Scenario tab of the CompositeProvider editor is designed to implement the actual logical layer. On this tab, you can specify the source PartProviders and define the proper operations to get the desired output, according to the required business logic. Figure 1-36 shows the Scenario tab of the CompositeProvider editor.

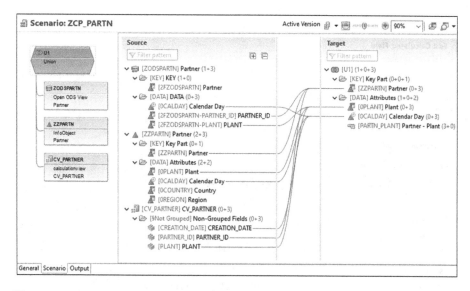

Figure 1-36. *CompositeProvider, Scenario tab*

In my example, I combined data from three different objects: Open
ODS View object (ZODSPARTN), InfoObject (ZZPARTN), and calculation
view (CV_PARTNER). The union operator combines data sets from all
the underlying objects and maps its fields from the source to the target
structure (Figure 1-36). In the target structure of CompositeProvider there
are three InfoObjects: Partner (ZZPARTN), Plant (0PLANT), and Calendar
Day (0CALDAY). Although the objects CV_PARTNER and ZODSPARTN
consist of raw fields (except 0CALDAY in Open ODS View), I was able to
map them to the target InfoObjects. In Figure 1-36 you can also notice
that the field PARTN_PLANT has no associations to PartProviders. This
is a calculated column, which can be created by right-clicking the Target
section and selecting Create Calculated Field. The Calculated Field editor
will open in a new window, as shown in Figure 1-37.

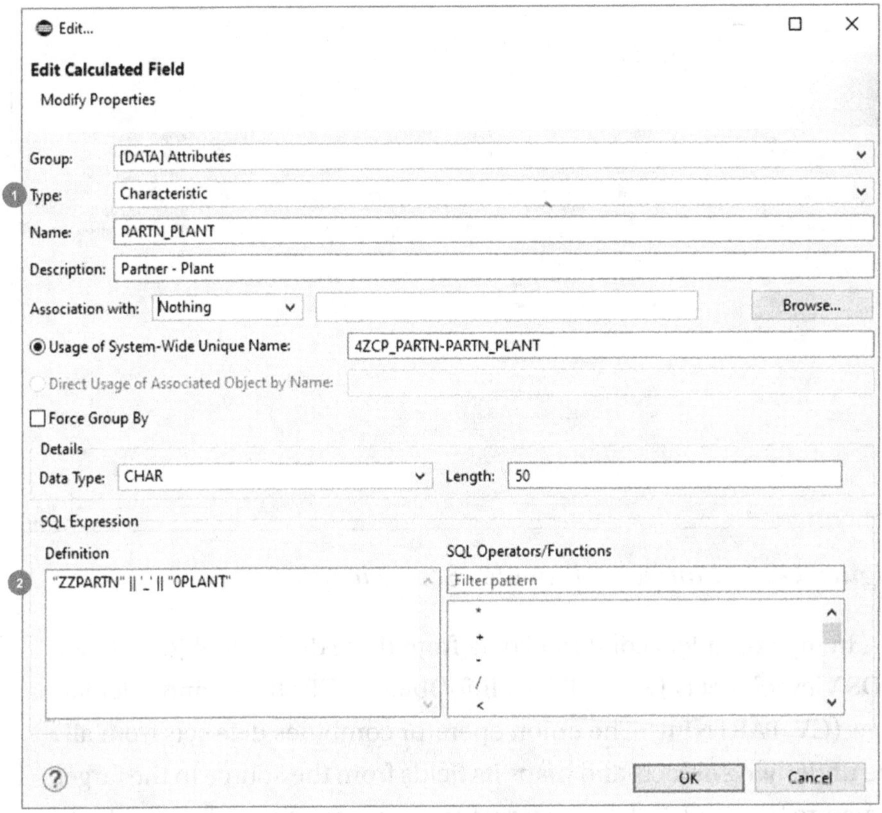

Figure 1-37. CompositeProvider, Calculated Field editor

In the Calculated Field editor, first we should define the field type: choose Characteristic or Key Figure depending on whether it is a dimension or a measure. We should also provide a name and description for the calculated field. It is possible to make an association between the calculated field and InfoObject or the Open ODS View object using the option "Association with." In my example, I kept this field without an association to the Master Data object. After specifying the data type, in the Definition section we can type a SQL expression. As shown in Figure 1-37, I used the following SQL syntax:

```
"ZZPARTN" || '_' || "0PLANT"
```

This expression concatenates the Partner and Plant InfoObject values, putting an underscore in between. I recommend you always test the code in the SQL console (SAP HANA modeler perspective) to verify if it works and returns the desired result.

Note When creating the calculated field, in the SQL expression you can refer only to the columns that are available in the Target section of the CompositeProvider structure. Moreover, each field specified in the expression should be enclosed in double quotes (i.e., "OPLANT").

The last tab available in the CompositeProvider editor is the Output tab (Figure 1-38).

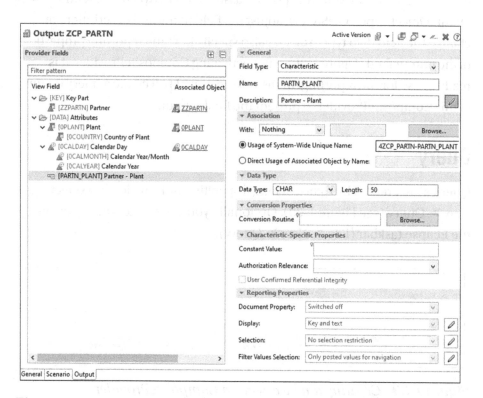

Figure 1-38. CompositeProvider, Output tab

In the left pane of the CompositeProvider Output tab, there is a Provider Fields section where you can find all the fields added to the output in the Scenario tab. In addition to the listed fields, you can enable for reporting the navigation attributes of specific InfoObjects (if available). If you right-click InfoObject from the Provider Fields list, you will see the Navigation Attributes option (if there are no navigation attributes for the selected InfoObject, the option will be grayed out). After selecting this option, the Navigation Attributes window will appear, and you will be able to select these attributes. In the example shown in Figure 1-38, you can see that navigation attributes were added both for Plant (0COUNTRY) and for Calendar Day (0CALMONTH, 0CALYEAR).

The right pane of the Output tab is for setting the properties of the output fields. In this section, you can apply an association between a field and an InfoObject/Open ODS View, adjust the field name and description, or change the field data type. You can also specify here the reporting properties of the output field (Figure 1-38). After activating CompositeProvider, it is ready to use for the reporting. In the next section, I will create a query on top of this CompositeProvider to present the final output.

Query

Queries are created by right-clicking a specific InfoProvider and selecting New ➤ Query (see Figure 1-39). Optionally you can create a query using the Eclipse taskbar (File ➤ New ➤ Query).

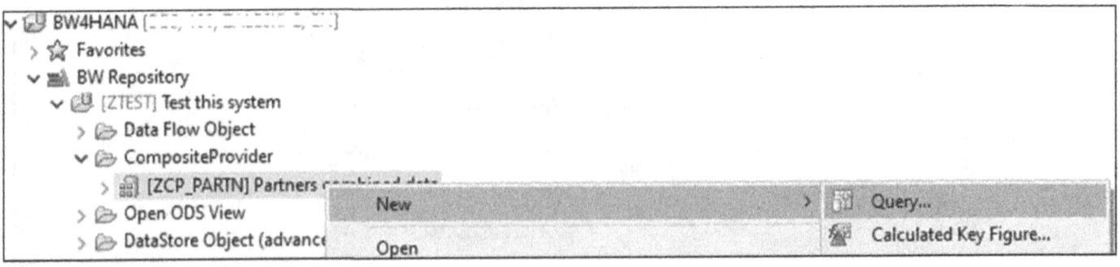

Figure 1-39. Creating a new query on CompositeProvider

On the first screen, as usual you need to provide a query technical name and optionally a description. Figure 1-40 shows the General tab of the query editor.

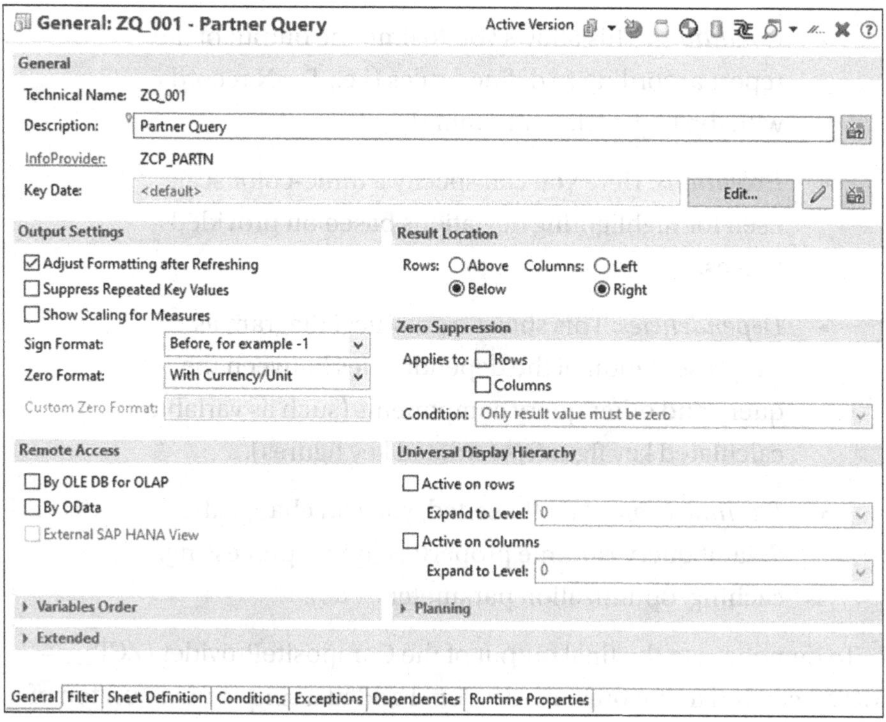

Figure 1-40. *Query, General tab*

Here is an overview of all the tabs available in the Query Designer (as in Figure 1-40).

- *General*: This tab is dedicated to setting general query properties (visibility to third-party tools, default display options, name, and description, etc.).

- *Filter*: This is used to set query filters and assign variables.

- *Sheet Definition*: This enables you to define a default report structure. Here you can specify a list of fields available for the reporting as well as define the default output structure.

- *Conditions*: This allows you to limit the output of the report according to defined rules (i.e., TopN records with the highest income value).

- *Exceptions*: Here you can specify a three-color scale used for highlighting deviations based on provided ranges.

- *Dependencies*: This shows a graphical diagram as a representation of the dependencies between the query and other query components (such as variables, calculated key figures, restricted key figures).

- *Runtime Properties*: If needed, you can change the default query runtime properties (query processing, caching, optimization parameters, etc.).

To demonstrate the final output of the CompositeProvider (ZCP_PARTN) created in the previous section, I added a simple query on top of it. Figure 1-41 shows the query definition.

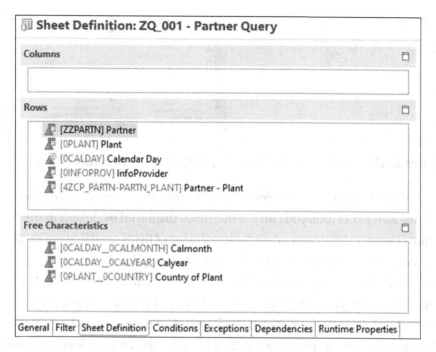

Figure 1-41. *Definition of a query on the CompositeProvider object ZCP_PARTN*

As shown in Figure 1-41, there are eight fields added to the output of the query ZQ_001. Five of them, available in the Rows section, will be displayed by default when opening the report. The three remaining fields are added to the Free Characteristics section. These will not be visible in the output of the report by default; however, the user will have the ability to add them if needed. Figure 1-42 shows the results of the query ZQ_001 in the SAP Analysis for Microsoft Excel front-end tool.

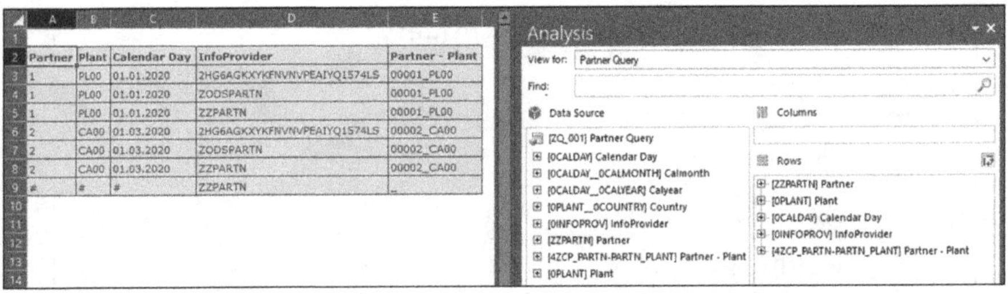

Figure 1-42. *Query ZQ_001 in SAP Analysis for Microsoft Office*

As defined in the Query object, when running the report in the Analysis for Microsoft Excel tool, you can see five fields displayed by default in the output (Figure 1-42). If you take a look at the list of fields available under the data source name, the remaining three are also available. In the previous section, I defined CompositeProvider as an union of three objects: HANA View, Open ODS View, and InfoObject. All three objects contain the same data, so you can notice that each record is displayed three times (except the # value, which exists only in InfoObject). The only differentiator for each record is the InfoProvider column, where you can find the source PartProvider information. Thanks to that column, you can easily identify the source object for each record. You may observe that for the calculation view, instead of its technical name, the value 2HG6AGKXYKFNVNVPEAIYQ1574LS is displayed. This is because BW/4HANA generates its own HANA views' technical identifiers, with names that always start with a 2H string.

Data Flow

There are multiple scenarios for using Data Flow objects. First, Data Flow objects can be used to model process flows. Before creating target BW/4HANA objects, you can create a Data Flow object to model your desired process. To create a Data Flow object, simply right-click the InfoArea and select New ➤ Data Flow Object. After providing the name of the object, the Data Flow editor will open (see Figure 1-43).

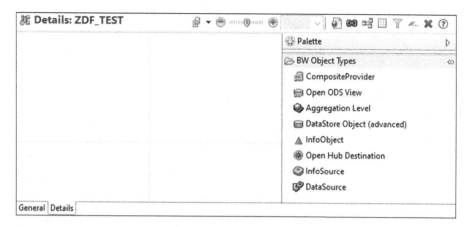

Figure 1-43. *Data Flow object editor*

In the right pane (Figure 1-43), you have the list of object types available for creating a process flow. You can add them to your model by using drag-and-drop functionality or by right-clicking the modeling area and selecting the New option. You can also include existing BW/4HANA objects in your model by selecting the Add Object option and providing the name of the object. After adding objects to the model, you can connect them using arrows to depict the dependencies. Figure 1-44 shows the exemplary data flow model.

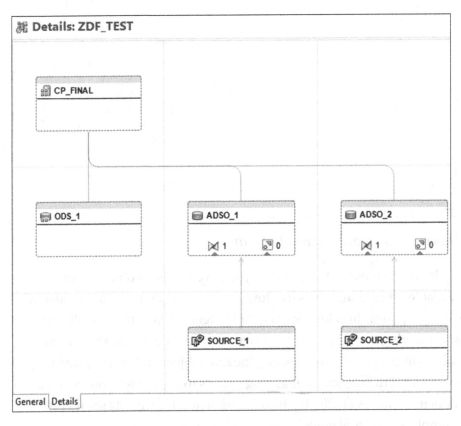

Figure 1-44. *Model created in the Data Flow object*

As shown in Figure 1-44, the data flow consists of two data sources (SOURCE_1 and SOURCE_2), which are linked with two ADSOs (ADSO_1 and ADSO_2). There is also one Open ODS View object (ODS_1) not linked to any data source. CompositeProvider (CP_FINAL) is modeled as a logical layer and combines data from Open ODS View and Advanced DSOs. Objects displayed in the Data Flow model are not associated with physical BW/4HANA objects. The created data flow model is just a template that can be later used as a reference for creating physical objects.

Another great usage of Data Flow objects is the ability to generate persistent objects out of data flow models. This means that after creating the process flow template, we can then convert objects from the model into physical BW/4HANA objects. It's always good to start from the objects at the bottom. Thanks to that, output structures can be propagated from the lower-level object to the upper one. After double-clicking the Data Source object, I can define its properties and activate it. Once that's done, the data flow diagram will be updated accordingly (see Figure 1-45).

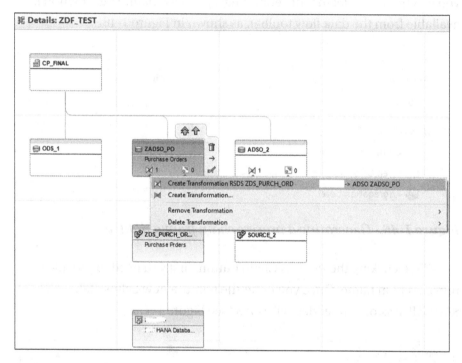

Figure 1-45. *Converting the data flow model into physical objects*

As shown in Figure 1-45, after creating a physical data source in place of the SOURCE_1 object, the model has been updated. Once the data source ZDS_PURCH_ORD was created, I clicked the ADSO_1 object and created the physical DataStore object called ZADSO_PO. The structure of that ADSO was inherited from the underlying data source. In Figure 1-45, I highlighted also the function for generating a transformation from the model. The same is possible for the DTP. This modeling approach allows you to first create a concept for your process and then convert this concept into the working solution. It can save time since generating objects from a data flow is a bit faster than creating them manually one by one from the Project Explorer.

If the Data Flow object consists fully of persistent BW/4HANA objects, you can utilize the feature of generating a process chain. This function is available from the data flow toolbar, as shown in Figure 1-46.

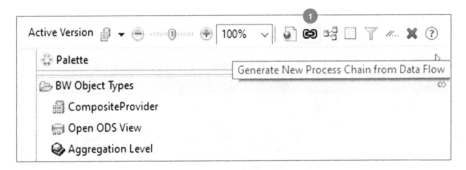

Figure 1-46. *Generating a process chain from a data flow*

When clicking the Process Chain button, first you need to provide a process chain name. Once you enter the name, a new Eclipse tab with a SAP GUI session embedded will open (see Figure 1-47).

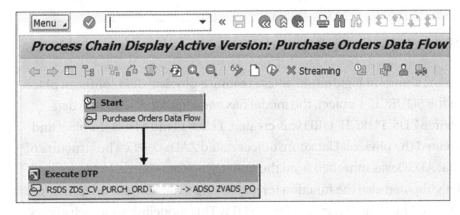

Figure 1-47. *Process chain window*

Figure 1-47 shows that the DTP from the data flow model has been automatically inserted into the process chain definition. If the Data Flow object is modified, the changes will not be automatically reflected in the process chain. You will need to incorporate these changes manually or generate a new process chain from the Data Flow object.

Data Flow objects can be also generated for existing BW/4HANA objects. To open a Data Flow object for a specific object, go to the Project Explorer list, right-click the object, and select the Explorer Data Flow option (Figure 1-48).

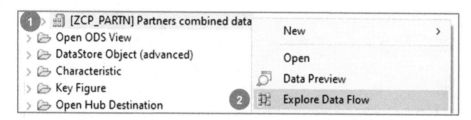

Figure 1-48. *Displaying a data flow for the existing object*

By default data flows for existing objects are opened as a collapsed view, so not all objects and dependencies may be visible. In the data flow editor you can expand the data flow downward or upward to see additional objects. When hovering over the specific node, you will see arrow symbols, which enable you to narrow down the data flow (Figure 1-49).

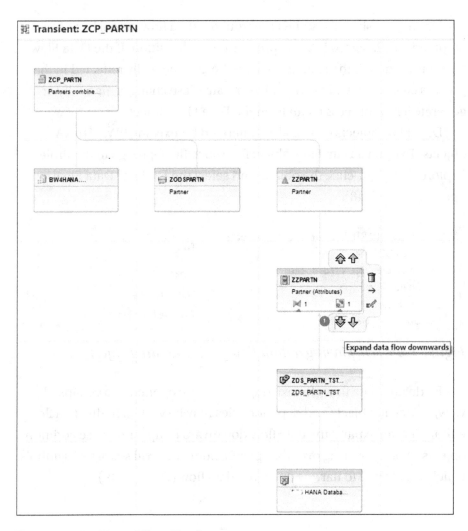

Figure 1-49. *Data Flow Explorer*

Figure 1-49 shows the data flow for the CompositeProvider named
ZCP_PARTN. It consists of three objects: Calculation View, Open ODS
View, and InfoObject. After expanding the data flow for the InfoObject
named ZZPARTN, we can see also Data Source and Source System used for
loading master data into InfoObject attributes. Worth mentioning is that
when you double-click a calculation view, in a new Eclipse tab the system

will open a definition of this calculation view (even though it is a HANA artifact and not BW/4HANA). Exploring data flow functionality can be useful when analyzing existing data flows.

The last feature that I want to highlight is the data flow documentation. This function enables possibility of describing role of each Data Flow node. Documentation can be added to both persistent and conceptual nodes. Figure 1-50 shows how to add documentation for a specific node.

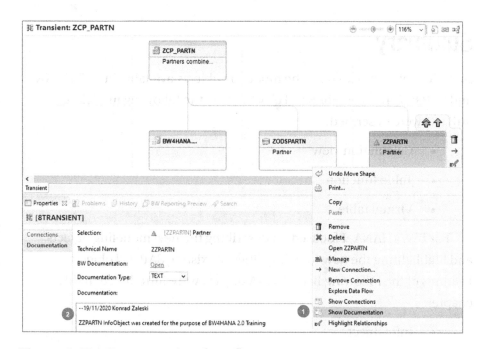

Figure 1-50. *Documenting data flows*

As shown in Figure 1-50, after right-clicking a specific node you can select the Show Documentation option. In the Documentation section there is an option to input any text describing a specific object. In the presented example, I added documentation for the ZZPARTN InfoObject node. This might help other developers to understand the entire process as well as the role of single objects.

Note   The entered documentation will be visible only in the context of a specific data flow. If you create a new data flow, the documentation section will be empty for all the nodes, even though some of the objects might be documented already within different data flows.

Summary

In this chapter, we explored the modeling objects available in SAP HANA and SAP BW/4HANA. For SAP HANA native, the following modeling artifacts were described:

- Calculation view

- Table function

- Virtual table

For BW/4HANA, I focused on describing the new modeling objects and highlighting the new functionalities of existing SAP BW objects. Features of the following BW/4HANA objects were introduced in this chapter:

- InfoObject

- Open ODS View

- Advanced DSO

- CompositeProvider

- Query

- Data Flow

CHAPTER 2

Modeling Concepts

In this chapter, I will describe the new modeling approaches introduced with SAP BW/4HANA. Not only does the new SAP business warehouse application significantly enhance the traditional SAP BW capabilities, but also it revolutionizes the modeling approach in general. This knowledge will be the key to understanding the new data warehousing functionalities, the bottom-up modeling approach, and the virtual data modeling concept.

Overview of SAP BW/4HANA Modeling Concepts

With the new functionalities and artifacts, BW/4HANA enables modern architecture based on the Layered Scalable Architecture++ (LSA++). This new architecture is leaner, simpler, and faster to implement. Moreover, it supports the virtualization approach, meaning that it may also be more cost effective.

LSA++ is an extension of the traditional LSA, which was available for SAP BW systems. In addition to reducing the number of modeling objects, LSA++ defines completely new standards for building data warehouses. Figure 2-1 presents the differences between the LSA and LSA++ approaches.

© Konrad Załęski 2021
K. Załęski, *Data Modeling with SAP BW/4HANA 2.0*,
https://doi.org/10.1007/978-1-4842-7089-9_2

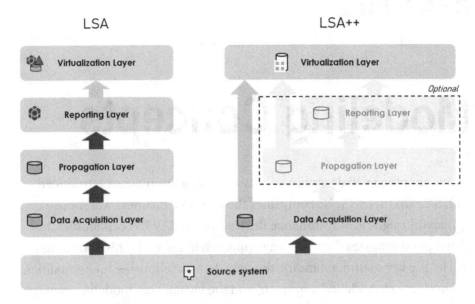

Figure 2-1. *Differences between LSA and LSA++*

As shown in Figure 2-1, the traditional LSA is based on several layers. On each of the layers, data is being physically stored, making the LSA architecture highly data redundant. Because of the high number of objects needing to be created, the maintenance of such an architecture is complex and not flexible. Lack of flexibility, high maintenance, and development effort all increase significantly the cost of the data warehouse. A high level of data redundancy and the top-down modeling approach both led to monolithic architectures that couldn't be used as part of the agile software development approach.

The SAP BW/4HANA environment introduces the new, modern LSA++ architecture, which is heavily focused on virtual objects. As shown in Figure 2-1, there is no need to create several staging layers and copy data from one layer to another. Virtual data marts can now be built directly on top of the data acquisition layer. If there is more than one staging layer needed, CompositeProviders can virtually combine data across the layers. Another virtualization capability is creating reports on top of virtual tables that physically reside in different databases. This means that reporting can be done without loading external data into a SAP database (of course, this can cause performance issues for very large datasets).

Persistent layers supported by ADSOs can be defined using InfoObjects, but also by using field-based modeling, which significantly accelerates the development. Thanks to this approach, developers can quickly create a persistent layer and, if needed, later enrich the model by associating Master Data objects at the CompositeProvider level.

SAP BW/4HANA and the new LSA++ architecture gives much more flexibility and significantly reduces the maintenance, data storage, and development time. In this chapter, I will present the general modeling concepts available in SAP BW/4HANA 2.0.

Note   The modeling concepts described in this chapter will highlight BW/4HANA 2.0 functionalities and features. Be aware that there is no single recommended architecture for all scenarios. It is also not possible to cover all the possible approaches; hence, I will visualize the ones that I find to be common. The discussion of the concepts will be followed by examples in the next chapters of this book.

Traditional Data Models

Traditional BW modeling follows a top-down approach, where before creating any model it is required to create an InfoObject for every single output field. Figure 2-2 shows a high-level approach for creating a classic EDW in BW/4HANA.

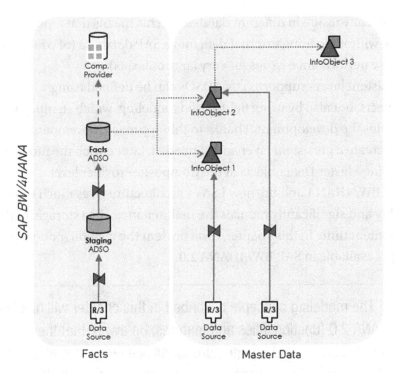

Figure 2-2. *BW/4HANA classic modeling concept*

Figure 2-2 shows a simplified scenario for the classic BW modeling approach. The diagram can be also used as a reference for comparing the classic approach with the new agile modeling concepts.

In the classic modeling approach, before creating transactional ADSOs, we need to first define the attributes, key figures, and master data InfoObjects. In Figure 2-2, you might notice the link between InfoObject 2 and InfoObject 3. This is because that master data InfoObject consists of attributes and navigational attributes. Before we are able to implement even a draft version of our data model, we need to first create all elementary building blocks in the form of InfoObjects. As shown in Figure 2-2, the Facts ADSO is modeled fully based on InfoObjects. Solid lines on the diagram indicate that data from data sources are loaded into target objects. On top of the ADSO there is a CompositeProvider, which allows us to combine data from multiple providers. Although we could create a BW Query object directly on ADSO, it is always better to take advantage of a CompositeProvider, which provides additional functionalities and gives us the ability to include other InfoProviders.

The classic BW/4HANA approach leads to a long development time and high maintenance effort. Despite its disadvantages, the classic approach is from my point of view still the fundamental way to implement an enterprise data warehouse for SAP data. In this approach, the data model relies on stable and reusable structures. Data persistency ensures a high-performing solution. In addition to adapting the SAP business content, we can take advantage of predefined data models. We can use them to jump-start delivering EDW solutions as well as a guideline for further development.

In the next part of this section, I will describe some new modeling concepts.

Note   Please be aware that in the following discussion of new modeling concepts, HANA physical tables and virtual tables can be utilized in the same way (even though sometimes only one table type will be presented in the diagram).

Virtual Data Provisioning

The first concept that I will introduce is reporting on SAP HANA artifacts. There might be a scenario where we want to simply enable the structure and the content of a SAP HANA physical table or virtual table in the BW/4HANA system. In Figure 2-3, you can see the concept of data provisioning directly from the HANA table.

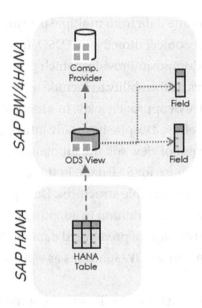

Figure 2-3. *BW/4HANA concept of table data provisioning*

The concept illustrated in Figure 2-3 shows how we can expose the HANA table through the BW/4HANA layer. In this approach, Open ODS View objects are the virtual BW/4HANA objects used as a layer between a CompositeProvider and a HANA table. They can be consumed by a CompositeProvider to provide the data from the underlying HANA table, without any data persistency. This concept takes advantage of a field-based approach, so we don't need to create any InfoObjects. All the fields can be simply dragged from the underlying table structure to the target structure of the Open ODS View object. The Open ODS View object can be then consumed by the CompositeProvider (optionally we could also create a query directly on top of the Open ODS View object). Dotted lines in the diagram indicate that the data flow is fully virtualized, so no data loads are required. Such requirements are pretty common for data extractions, ad hoc data analysis, or prototyping purposes.

The next concept is similar to the one shown in Figure 2-3; however, here as a source we utilize a virtual table, which physically resides outside of the HANA database (for example in a Microsoft SQL or Oracle database). Figure 2-4 describes the concept of virtual table data provisioning.

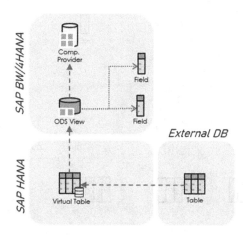

Figure 2-4. *BW/4HANA concept of virtual table data provisioning*

Using Smart Data Access (SDA), we can create a remote source connected to an external database. Once the remote source is configured, we will be able to create in the HANA system a virtual table with the same structure as the source table residing in the external database. The Open ODS View object enables us to source data directly both from a HANA table and from a virtual table. In the diagram shown in Figure 2-4, the Open ODS View object is created on top of the virtual table.

In scenarios when we need to apply some additional data manipulations on a source table or create a dataset that combines data from multiple tables (both virtual and regular), we can take advantage of calculation view capabilities (see Figure 2-5).

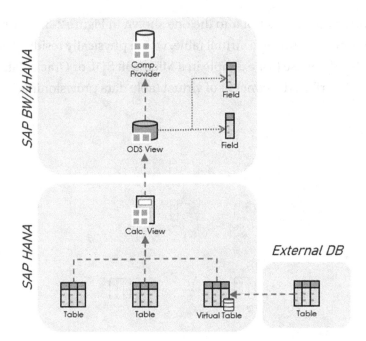

Figure 2-5. *BW/4HANA concept of calculation view data provisioning*

The variant depicted in Figure 2-5 is similar to the previous ones. The difference is only on the SAP HANA level, where there is a calculation view added on top of three tables. This calculation view combines data from the HANA tables and the virtual table. The BW/4HANA part remains the same as in the previous example, meaning from the calculation view, data is passed through a field-based Open ODS View object to the CompositeProvider object.

Note   It is possible to add a calculation view directly as the source of CompositeProvider. However, when creating an Open ODS View object, we also define a reusable logical object, with all the properties, structures, or associations to Master Data objects. Therefore, we don't need to apply all these settings every time when utilizing a specific calculation view as a source of a CompositeProvider object.

Field-Based Data Models

Let's now consider a more complex scenario, where the requirement is to create a snowflake data model in BW/4HANA based on data from HANA tables. Figure 2-6 presents a simple snowflake data model, which I will use as a reference for visualizing the BW/4HANA modeling approach.

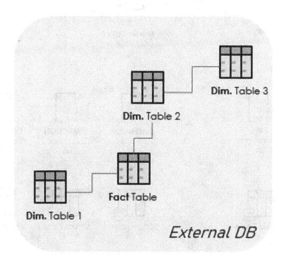

Figure 2-6. *Simplified snowflake schema*

The snowflake schema consists of a central fact table connected to multiple dimensions in a normalized form. To imitate the same behavior in BW/4HANA, we can again take advantage of Open ODS View objects. When creating Open ODS View objects, we have the option to indicate the type of the underlying object. We can define semantics as Facts, Master Data, or Text. Figure 2-7 visualizes an approach for implementing a virtual model in BW/4HANA, based on tables in HANA (see Figure 2-6).

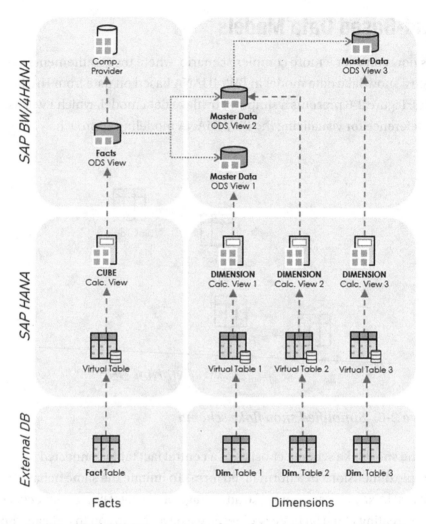

Figure 2-7. *BW/4HANA concept of implementing Open ODS View–based virtual model*

As shown in Figure 2-7, the data flows for facts and for dimensions are similar. For the fact table, there is a calculation view of the CUBE data category created, while for dimension tables it is view of the DIMENSION category. The same approach could be followed when utilizing physical tables residing directly in the HANA database.

Note   Virtual tables can be consumed by Open ODS Views directly, so it is not mandatory to create a calculation view as an intermediate layer. Nevertheless, I recommend creating calculation views, since this gives you flexibility if in the future you need to implement additional formatting, convert data types, or add calculated columns, which are quite common requirements.

For Open ODS View objects, there are also two semantic types used: Facts for fact tables and Master Data for three dimension tables. You may notice that Open ODS View 2 is linked to Open ODS View 3. This is to visualize that the Open ODS View 2 field has an association to the Open ODS View 3 master data. To better understand this concept, you can think about them as InfoObjects with attributes. You create a main InfoObject and specify a list of InfoObjects as navigational attributes. The only difference is that instead of using InfoObjects, you utilize Open ODS Views. The dotted line between the Facts Open ODS View and Master Data Open ODS View 1 and 2 also depicts an association of Fact Table fields with Master Data. The final CompositeProvider may still contain raw fields; however, there will be associations with Open ODS View master data objects. This approach enables you to create a snowflake data model without data persistency.

The modeling variant described in Figure 2-7 is fully virtualized and may not be suitable for complex data models or in scenarios were large data volumes need to be handled. In virtual data models, all the operations are performed on the fly, which obviously can lead to a performance decrease. In addition, virtual tables query data from external databases, which is also not efficient.

If you developed an Open ODS View object–based virtual data model and you realized that the performance is not good enough, you can automatically generate a persistent layer for selected Open ODS View objects (Facts and/or Master Data). Figure 2-8 shows the architecture of a persistent Open ODS View–based data model.

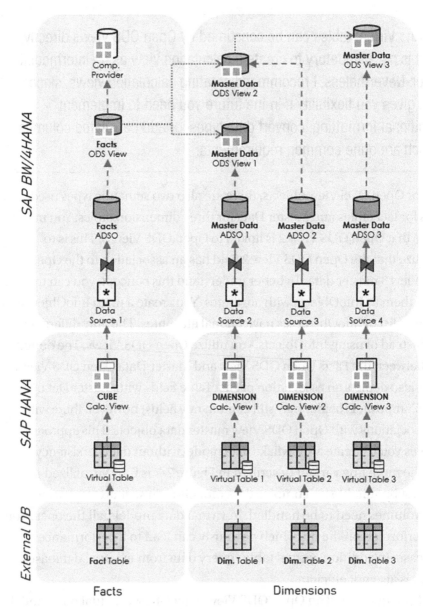

Figure 2-8. BW/4HANA concept of implementing Open ODS View–based persistent model

Open ODS Views provide functionality for generating data flows. With this functionality between the source object and the Open ODS View objects, the system generates the Data Source and ADSO as well as the transformation with DTP. When you compare the architecture in Figure 2-7 with Figure 2-8, you will notice that between the calculation view and the Open ODS View object there are two additional objects. A solid line indicates that data coming from the data source is physically loaded into the ADSO object using transformation and DTP. Of course, while analyzing your model from the performance improvement perspective, you can decide which Open ODS View objects require physical data storage. You don't need to choose between the virtual and persistent models, but you can selectively choose for which Open ODS Views you want to create a persistent ADSO layer. Usually because of the high data volume (millions of records), performance is mainly impacted for transactional tables. In this case, you can generate an ADSO for fact tables and keep the master data model virtual.

Hybrid Data Models

The next modeling variant is a combination of multiple modeling objects. As already mentioned in BW/4HANA, we are not forced to choose a single way of implementing the data model. BW/4HANA enables a hybrid modeling concept, where we can leverage InfoObjects, Open ODS View objects, and a field-based approach within a single data model. The hybrid approach can be used when parts of the dimensions from the newly created data model are consistent with the SAP master data. For example, in a production company, a plant naming convention could be standardized across all the systems. If this is the case, then while creating a new model in BW/4HANA, there is no point in creating and storing the same master data; we could utilize a standard 0PLANT InfoObject instead. As a result of adapting existing InfoObjects, we can take advantage of all their features such as attributes, navigational attributes, hierarchies, or authorization capabilities (for authorization-relevant InfoObjects).

Moreover, by adapting existing InfoObjects wherever it's possible, we ensure integrity and consistency as well as avoid redundancy and limit the development and maintenance effort. Figure 2-9 depicts the hybrid modeling approach in BW/4HANA.

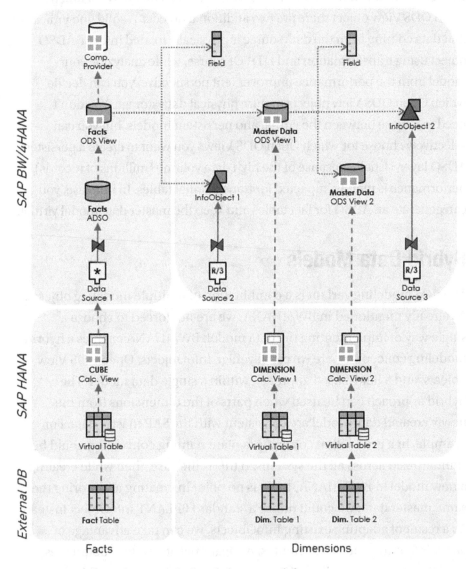

Figure 2-9. *BW/4HANA hybrid data model*

As shown in Figure 2-9, the Facts Open ODS View object is modeled based on three object types: InfoObject, Open ODS View, and Field. InfoObjects can be leveraged for dimensions, which have the same master data as in the SAP model. Some organizations might be using the master data management system; hence, multiple systems can share the same master data. If this is the case, some of the dimensions from the external data model could be mapped to SAP InfoObjects. It is good to utilize InfoObjects for external models whenever it's possible. This way, we provide additional attributes, without any development effort.

The second Facts Open ODS View building block used in Figure 2-9 is the Master Data Open ODS View. For the master data, the Open ODS View approach is the same as in the previous two models (Figures 2-7 and 2-8). In addition, when creating the Master Data Open ODS View, you have the possibility to associate fields with other Master Data Open ODS View objects, InfoObjects, or fields. Although the hybrid model gives dozens of combinations for designing the architecture, before the actual implementation I suggest you analyze in detail the entire data model (tables, fields, and relationships). Based on that, you can prepare the general approach and use cases for using each type of the object. My recommendation for hybrid modeling is as follows:

- Use InfoObjects whenever applicable (both for the Facts and Master Data Open ODS View objects).

- For non-SAP dimensions, create Master Data Open ODS Views.

- Create an ADSO only if the performance is not sufficient when leveraging virtual objects.

- If the InfoObject or Master Data Open ODS View association is not applicable, use a field-based approach.

- In the design phase, define the general architecture for the hybrid model and follow that approach (otherwise, the model can become complex and unmanageable).

The hybrid modeling concept can be used as a final architecture for virtual model implementation. Nevertheless, you need to remember that despite the Master Data Open ODS Views acting as virtual InfoObjects, this does not cover all their functionalities. A common requirement is the creation of hierarchies. Open ODS Views do not support hierarchies, while InfoObjects do. Another limitation is the transitive attributes functionality, which is also not available for Open ODS Views. In such a scenario, assuming that you want to keep your architecture virtual, you might take advantage of "virtual" InfoObjects. By "virtual" InfoObjects, I mean InfoObjects with the Access Type option set as SAP HANA View. Figure 2-10 shows the concept of a data model using HANA View–based InfoObjects.

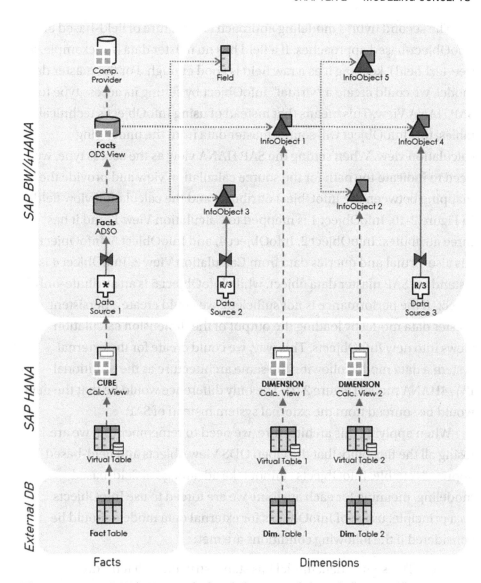

Figure 2-10. BW/4HANA hybrid data model with "virtual" InfoObjects

The second hybrid modeling approach is a mixture of field-based and InfoObject-based approaches. If a field has no master data (for example, a free-text field), keeping it as a raw field is good enough. For the master data model, we could create a "virtual" InfoObject by setting its access type to SAP HANA View. This means that instead of using InfoObject's technical tables, this InfoObject will source master data from the underlying calculation view. When setting the SAP HANA view as the access type, we need to indicate the path for the source calculation view and provide the mapping between the InfoObject attributes and the calculation view fields. In Figure 2-10, InfoObject 1 is mapped to Calculation View 1, and it has three attributes: InfoObject 2, InfoObject 4, and InfoObject 5. InfoObject 2 is also virtual and queries data from Calculation View 2. InfoObject 4 is a standard SAP master data object, while InfoObject 5 is an attribute-only object. If the performance is not sufficient, we could create a persistent master data model by loading the output of the dimension calculation views into new InfoObjects. This way, we could create for the external system a data model following the same architecture as the traditional BW/4HANA model (Figure 2-2). The only difference would be that the data would be sourced from the external system instead of SAP.

When applying this architecture, we need to remember that we are losing all the flexibility that the Open ODS View objects and field-based approach enable. InfoObjects cannot take advantage of field-based modeling, meaning for each attribute we are forced to use InfoObjects. As a principle, usage of InfoObjects for external data models should be considered if the following conditions are met:

- The source data model has stable structures that hardly change.

- In the pilot phase, you created a field-based model that was tested, and as a next iteration, you want to convert it to a structured model followed by the classic BW/4HANA modeling concept.

- There is a need for leveraging functionality that is not available for Open ODS Views or fields. In this case, use a "virtual" InfoObject for these specific dimensions (i.e., when a hierarchy is required).

Best practice   Performance may not be sufficient when the data model is fully based on virtual tables (the model used on HANA physical tables will have better performance). If the source model consists of huge fact tables and multiple dimension tables, data persistency will be required.

Figure 2-11 shows the architecture of a hybrid data model using persistent InfoObjects.

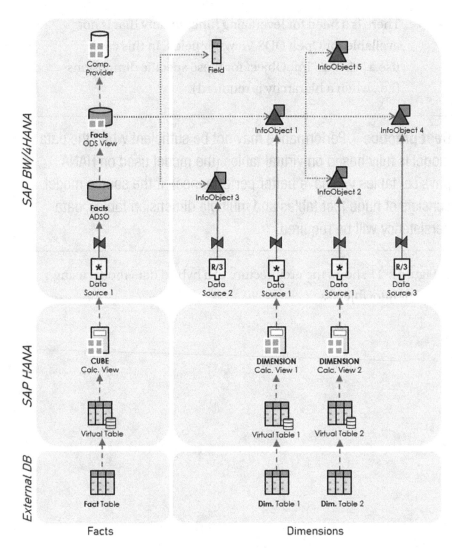

Figure 2-11. *BW/4HANA hybrid data model with persistent InfoObjects*

The architecture shown in Figure 2-11 is similar to the classic modeling concept (Figure 2-2). The difference is that custom InfoObjects (InfoObject 1 and InfoObject 2) are loaded with data coming from the external system instead of the SAP system. With this approach all the InfoObject functionalities can be leveraged for external master data, and performance will not be impacted. On the other hand, development and maintenance require a higher effort. When analyzing the architecture shown in Figure 2-11, you can ask yourself, why instead of creating a new model could I not simply load non-SAP data into the existing SAP data model structures?

You might be thinking about the approach shown in Figure 2-12.

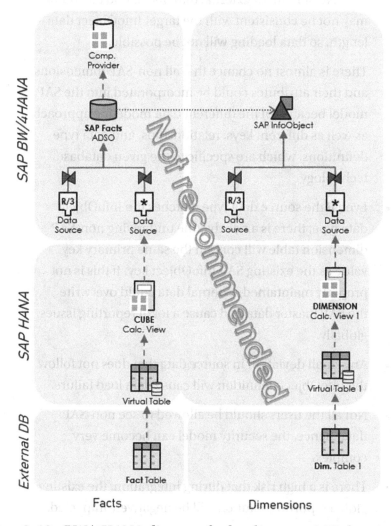

Figure 2-12. *BW/4HANA diagram for loading non-SAP data into the SAP data model*

The approach for including external data into the existing SAP data model has the following limitations:

- The data type for external dimensions and attributes may not be consistent with the target InfoObject data type, so data loading will not be possible.

- The data length for external dimension and attributes may not be consistent with the target InfoObject data length, so data loading will not be possible.

- There is almost no chance that all non-SAP dimensions and their attributes could be incorporated into the SAP model because of the different data modeling approach as well as different keys, relationships, and data type definitions, which are specific to the given database technology.

- Even if the source data type matches the InfoObject data type, there is a risk that the underlying non-SAP dimension table will contain the same primary key value as the existing SAP InfoObject key. If this is not properly maintained, external data could overwrite the SAP master data and cause a lot of reporting issues globally.

- Any small deviation in source data that does not follow the InfoObject definition will cause data load failure.

- Not all the users should be allowed to see non-SAP data; hence, the security model can become very complex.

- There is a high risk that during integration, the existing global reporting solution will be negatively impacted.

With all these limitations and disadvantages, we can say that there is no easy way to integrate external data into an existing SAP data warehouse. Nevertheless, we can create a new data model, which will combine SAP and non-SAP data.

Combined Data Models (SAP and Non-SAP Data)

In scenarios where we want to combine SAP and non-SAP data into a single data model, by leveraging virtualization capabilities we can avoid data redundancy (meaning storing the same SAP data twice in both models). Having in mind all the functionalities available in BW/4HANA, creating a combined model could follow multiple different approaches. Figure 2-13 shows one of the approaches for integrating SAP and non-SAP data into a single model.

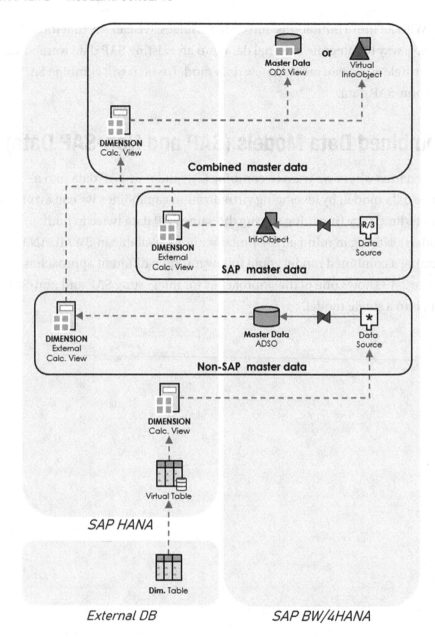

Figure 2-13. *BW/4HANA integration of SAP and non-SAP master data into the new model*

Figure 2-13 shows the architecture for creating a master data object that combines data from SAP and non-SAP dimensions. The diagram highlights three sections with SAP, non-SAP, and combined master data. For non-SAP data, there is a Master Data ADSO as the persistent layer created. As you might already know, BW/4HANA gives the ability to autogenerate an external SAP HANA view out of modeling objects. This functionality is leveraged in this approach. Out of the Master Data ADSO, there is an external calculation view generated. The same functionality is used for the SAP master data, meaning that for SAP InfoObject, an external calculation view is also generated. Once we have both datasets available on the HANA platform in the form of external calculation views, we can combine them into single dimension view. As shown in Figure 2-13, on top of two external views, there is an additional calculation view created. The purpose of that view is to union SAP and non-SAP data.

Note   You can avoid creating a persistent master data ADSO for non-SAP data and combine an external view generated from an InfoObject with the virtual table directly. This approach, however, will have a negative impact on the data model's performance.

Of course, when combining SAP and non-SAP data, some of the attributes may be available only for SAP, while others are for only non-SAP sources. To mitigate user confusion, if an attribute value is missing or it's just not available for a specific record, it would be good to include in the data model field for indicating the source system for each record. In a combined calculation view, you will be able to apply additional data manipulations to unify both datasets as much as possible. In addition, before being able to apply mapping in calculation view union node, it is likely that you will need to convert values to the common data types first. Once you have your combined master data properly shaped, you will be able to consume the final master data view either with a master data Open ODS View or with an InfoObject of SAP HANA View access type (depending on the approach).

Following the approach for integrating master data, we can apply the same architecture for the fact data. Figure 2-14 depicts the architecture of integrating SAP and non-SAP data into the new BW/4HANA model.

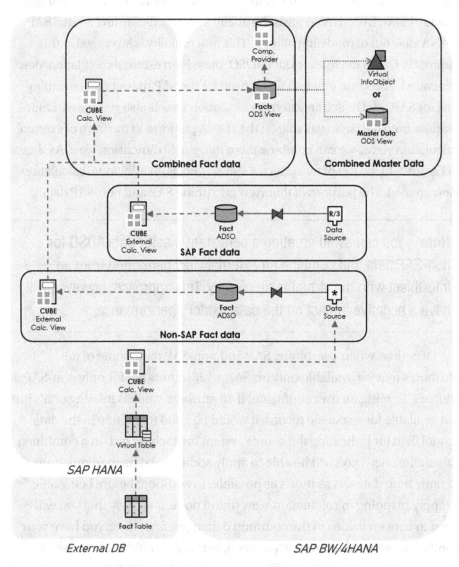

Figure 2-14. *BW/4HANA integration of SAP and non-SAP data into a new model*

The architecture for integrating the fact data follows the same approach as the integration of the master data. The difference is that the external calculation views are generated from fact ADSOs (both for SAP and for non-SAP data). External calculation views generated out of ADSOs are combined with the union operator within the calculation view created on top. The final calculation view with the combined fact data will be later consumed by the Facts Open ODS View. As shown in Figure 2-14, in the Open ODS View object, the fields derived from the underlying calculation view are associated with the combined Master Data objects (described in Figure 2-13). Depending on the chosen approach, the fields can be mapped to Master Data Open ODS Views or "virtual" InfoObjects. Some of the fields can be also kept without any associations. The CompositeProvider created on top of the Facts Open ODS View can be later consumed with the final query.

As you can see, there are many possible modeling concepts, and depending on the requirements, you need to choose the most appropriate approach. Remember that the architectures described in this chapter are not the only possible variants. There are many more architectures that could be designed. BW/4HANA simplifies modeling by limiting the number of objects and layers, but with all the new features and functionalities it enables much more possible modeling approaches; hence, choosing the most appropriate architecture for a given scenario can be really challenging. The keys for designing the right model are deep requirements and data model analysis, timeline for project delivery, and developer experience.

Summary

This chapter explained the concepts of utilizing BW/4HANA and HANA native objects to implement agile data models consuming data from HANA physical and virtual tables. Table 2-1 summarizes the pros, cons, and usage for each of the modeling concepts covered in this chapter.

Table 2-1. *Comparison of Modeling Concepts*

Traditional Data Models	
Pros	• High level of data stability, quality, and consistency
	• Possibility of using SAP business content
	• Access managed by the security model
Cons	• Low flexibility, strict development rules
	• Suitable mainly for SAP data
	• High development and maintenance effort
	• Data persistency always required
Usage	• SAP data models

Virtual Data Provisioning	
Pros	• High flexibility
	• Very low development effort
	• Easy to implement and maintain
	• No need for creating InfoObjects
	• Data persistency not required
Cons	• No master data
	• Provides only specific piece of information
	• Security model not applicable (unless association to InfoObjects in maintained)
Usage	• Simple data provisioning/extractions
	• Ad hoc analysis
	• Direct access to virtual tables

(*continued*)

Table 2-1. (*continued*)

Field-Based Data Models	
Pros	• High flexibility • Easy to implement and maintain • No need to create InfoObjects • Data persistency optional • Possible to implement authorization model
Cons	• Open ODS View objects not supporting all InfoObjects features (i.e., hierarchies) • For complex data models, performance lower
Usage	• Non-SAP data models
Hybrid Data Models	
Pros	• High flexibility • No need to create new InfoObjects • Possibility of utilizing existing master data objects where applicable • Access managed by the security model
Cons	• Without strict modeling guidelines, by mixing many objects from different areas, model may become complex and difficult to maintain • For complex data models, performance may be not sufficient
Usage	• Non-SAP data models having dimensions that correspond to SAP master data

(*continued*)

Table 2-1. (*continued*)

Combined Data Models	
Pros	• Gives users possibility to run data analytics and reporting on global data (SAP and non-SAP) • Authorization model can be implemented
Cons	• Design of the combined model requiring detailed and time-consuming analysis • Complex implementation • Generates a lot of dependencies through external SAP HANA views, which may negatively affect SAP models • Pretty high maintenance effort
Usage	• Integration of SAP and non-SAP data into a single model

The concepts described in this chapter give you an idea of how to provision external table data into BW/4HANA, implement reports and data models based on non-SAP tables, and integrate SAP and non-SAP data into a single data model. In the next chapters, by using examples, you will learn how to implement these concepts in BW/4HANA systems.

CHAPTER 3

Publishing HANA Objects Through BW/4HANA

In this chapter, I will go through different scenarios where data residing in HANA needs to be published through the BW/4HANA reporting layer. You will get a practical guide for exposing HANA tables and HANA calculation views to the BW/4HANA system. Moreover, I will show how you can pass values that were input on the Query Variable level directly to the calculation view and table function input parameter.

The appendix contains some SQL scripts that can be used for creating table structures and populating them with exemplary data. For demonstration purposes, I will use these tables, so if you want to follow the scenarios described in this chapter, you can use the same source objects in your system.

Publish HANA Tables Through BW/4HANA

CASE STUDY 1

Company XYZ is using the BW/4HANA system as the main reporting platform. Reports created in BW/4HANA are later consumed by the Analysis for Microsoft Excel for Microsoft Office and SAP Analytics Cloud (SAC) front-end tools.

© Konrad Załęski 2021
K. Załęski, *Data Modeling with SAP BW/4HANA 2.0*,
https://doi.org/10.1007/978-1-4842-7089-9_3

Company XYZ evaluates the possibility of integrating external data into the SAP reporting platform to be able to utilize both SAP and non-SAP data in the Analysis for Microsoft Excel and SAC tools. In the pilot phase, Company XYZ decided to enable a single transactional table with external data. The table named ORDER_HEADER is populated with data related to orders that come from the non-SAP system. The requirement is to enable data from this HANA table for reporting into the BW/4HANA platform. The structure of the final query should be the same as the structure of the source table. Table 3-1 describes the details of the source table structure.

Table 3-1. *Structure of the ORDER_HEADER Table*

Column Name	Key	Data Type	Description
ORD_NUMBER	X	VARCHAR(10)	Order number
DOC_DATE		DATE	Document date
REQ_DATE		DATE	Requested delivery date
SHIP_DATE		DATE	Ship date
DELV_DATE		DATE	Delivery date
STATUS		VARCHAR(3)	Order status
CUST_NUMBER		VARCHAR(10)	Customer number
EMP_NUMBER		VARCHAR(10)	Employee number
FREE_TEXT		VARCHAR(5000)	Comments

Table ORDER_HEADER consists of nine columns. The primary key, which uniquely identifies each record, is the ORD_NUMBER column and contains order numbers. The rest of the columns contain order header information such as the status, document date, or customer number.

Note   Refer to the book's appendix if you want to re-create the
ORDER_HEADER table structure and populate it with data in your SAP
HANA system.

In this scenario, I will follow the modeling concept that was illustrated
in Figure 2-3 of Chapter 2. Figure 3-1 presents the detailed approach that I
will follow to fulfill the requirements from Case Study 1.

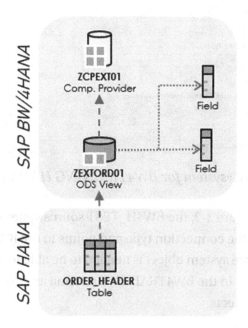

Figure 3-1. *Publishing HANA tables through BW/4HANA (Case
Study 1)*

From the BW/4HANA side, the table ORDER_HEADER will be
consumed by an Open ODS View object. On top of that Open ODS View, I
will create a CompositeProvider object (as shown in Figure 3-1). Once the
modeling objects are created, I will consume the CompositeProvider with
the Query object.

Create the Source System

To fulfill the requirements from Case Study 1, we do not need to create any additional objects on the HANA level. The only prerequisite for sourcing data from HANA is to create a dedicated source system object in the BW/4HANA system with SAP HANA's local database schema connection type. This source system should point to the schema where the target tables are stored. See Figure 3-2 as a reference.

General: BW4H_TEST

Source System	
Source System:	BW4H_TEST
Description:	Training schema

General Properties

Business Content Type and Release Assignment (optional):   Browse...

Specific Properties

Connection Type	Access to local HANA Schema
Owner/Schema	BW4TRAINING

Figure 3-2. *Source system for BW4TRAINING HANA schema*

As shown in Figure 3-2, the BW4H_TEST source system uses the local HANA schema as the connection type and points to the BW4TRAINING schema. This source system object is needed to be able to access the HANA tables stored in the BW4TRAINING schema and consume them via Open ODS View objects.

Create the Open ODS View Object for the Order-Header Data

Tables residing in the HANA database can be directly consumed by Open ODS Views in BW/4HANA. To create a new Open ODS View object, go to the target InfoArea and select New ➤ Open ODS View (Figure 3-3).

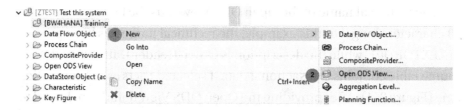

Figure 3-3. *Creating a new Open ODS View for the ORDER_ HEADER table*

As shown in Figure 3-3, the Open ODS View will be created under the BW/4HANA InfoArea. In the next step, you will be asked to provide the details of the Open ODS View object such as the technical name, description, and semantics. Figure 3-4 displays the initial properties of the Open ODS View object.

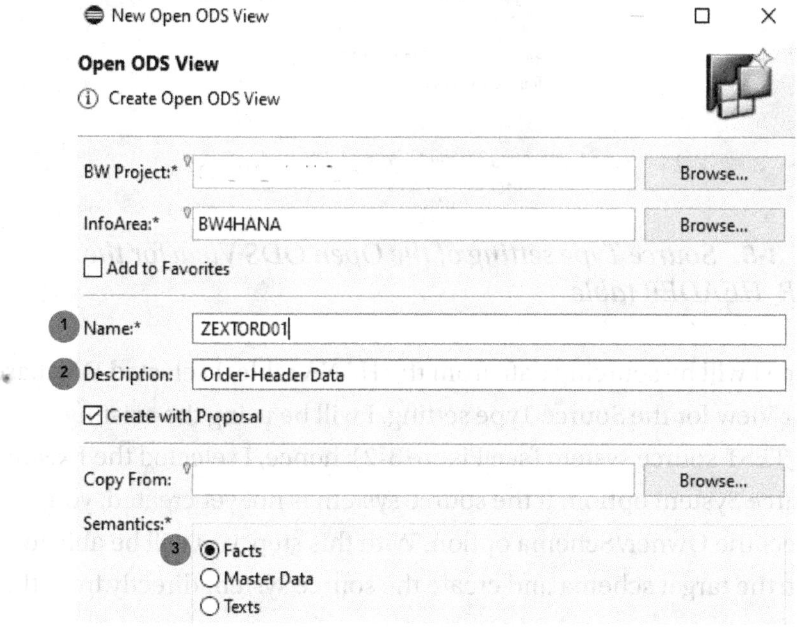

Figure 3-4. *Properties of the Open ODS View for the ORDER_ HEADER table*

101

The technical name of the Open ODS View must be between 3 and
28 characters long. For this example, the technical name has been set
to ZEXTORD01, while the description is Order-Header Data. Since the
source table contains transactional data, I selected Facts as the semantics
type (Figure 3-4). After providing the Open ODS View definition, I need to
indicate the proper Source Type setting, as in Figure 3-5.

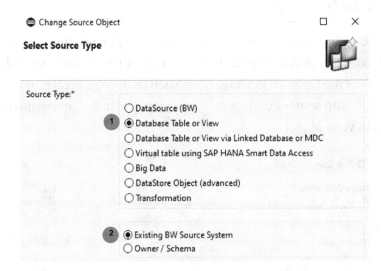

Figure 3-5. *Source Type setting of the Open ODS View for the*
ORDER_HEADER table

Since I will be sourcing data from the HANA table, I selected Database
Table or View for the Source Type setting. I will be using the existing
BW4H_TEST source system (see Figure 3-2); hence, I selected the Existing
BW Source System option. If the source system is not yet created, you
can select the Owner/Schema option. With this step, you will be able to
indicate the target schema and create the source system directly from the
wizard.

Note   To be able to consume tables from any HANA schema, you need to grant schema access to the SAPABAP1 technical user. Otherwise, the schema will not be visible from BW/4HANA.

Run the following SQL script to grant schema access to the SAPABAP1 user:

```
GRANT SELECT ON SCHEMA "<schema name>" TO SAPABAP1
```

To finalize the creation of the Open ODS View object, you need to indicate the target table. Once all the information is provided, the system will open the General tab of the Open ODS View editor (see Figure 3-6).

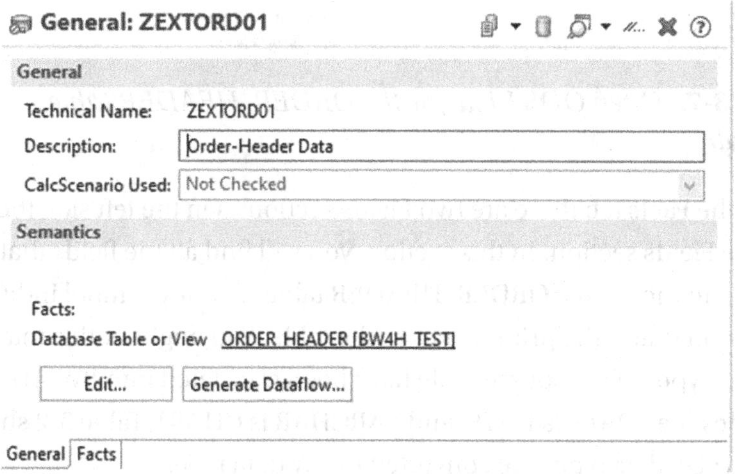

Figure 3-6. *Open ODS View for the ORDER_HEADER table, General tab*

On the General tab, you will find an overview of the Open ODS View object. The actual structure of the Open ODS View is defined on the Facts tab. On this tab, I need to define the output fields and their properties. In Figure 3-7 there is an output structure of the ZEXTORD01 Open ODS View object presented.

103

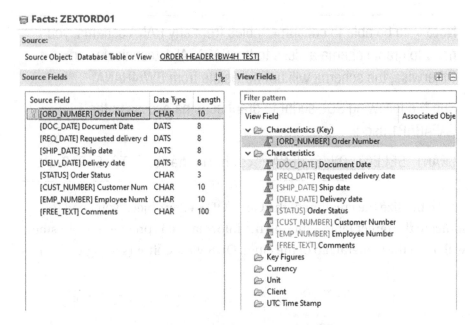

Figure 3-7. *Open ODS View for the ORDER_HEADER table, Facts tab*

On the Facts tab there are two Fields sections. On the left side there is a Source Fields section. In this section, you will find all the fields that are available in the source ORDER_HEADER table. The key symbol indicates the column that is the primary key of the table. You might notice that the SQL data types of the source table have been translated into BW/4HANA data types (i.e., DATE is DATS, and VARCHAR is CHAR). Table 3-2 shows how the SQL data types are converted to BW data types.

Table 3-2. *Mapping Between SQL Data Types and BW Data Types*

HANA SQL	BW/4HANA
DATE	DATS
TIME	TIMS
SECONDDATE	NUMC
TIMESTAMP	NUMC
TINYINT	INT1
SMALLINT	INT2
INTEGER	INT4
BIGINT	INT8
SMALLDECIMAL	FLTP
DECIMAL	DEC
REAL	FLTP
DOUBLE	FLTP
BOOLEAN	CHAR
VARCHAR	CHAR
NVARCHAR	CHAR
ALPHANUM	CHAR
SHORTTEXT	CHAR
VARBINARY	RAW
BLOB	*N/A*
CLOB	SSTR

(*continued*)

Table 3-2. (*continued*)

HANA SQL	BW/4HANA
NCLOB	SSTR
TEXT	SSTR
ST_GEOMETRY	CHAR
ST_POINT	CHAR

As shown in Table 3-2, not all SQL data types can be supported in the Open ODS View object. Large objects more than 1,333 characters long (i.e., the BLOB type or a VARCHAR longer than 1,333 characters) cannot be used in BW/4HANA objects.

On the right side of the pane (Figure 3-7) there is a View Fields section. In this section, you define the actual output structure of the Open ODS View. By default, the system created a structure proposal and assigned fields to specific groups. This is because of the Create with Proposal setting, which was selected when creating the Open ODS View (Figure 3-4). If needed, you can manually adjust the output structure by removing some fields or reassigning them to different groups. In my scenario, the ORD_ NUMBER column has been assigned to the Characteristics (Key) group, and the rest of the fields were grouped under the Characteristics catalog. Since this is the target structure and no adjustments are required, I will proceed with activating the ZEXTORD01 Open ODS View object.

Note   The unique field names of the Open ODS View are generated automatically and follow this pattern: 2F<Open ODS View name>-<Field Name>. The System-Wide Unique Name setting cannot be modified.

Create the CompositeProvider for the Order-Header Data

The Open ODS View object can be directly consumed by a query; however, as mentioned in Chapter 1, as a good practice it is better to create a CompositeProvider first. Therefore, in the future, you will be able to easily enhance the logical layer by combining additional providers or performing additional calculations. Follow the path shown in Figure 3-8 to create a new CompositeProvider.

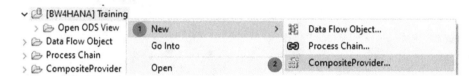

Figure 3-8. *Creating a new CompositeProvider for the ZEXTORD01 Open ODS View*

Once the technical name and description of CompositeProvider are provided, we can specify the default node and source providers. In our case, we will use the ZEXTORD01 Open ODS View as a PartProvider object (Figure 3-9).

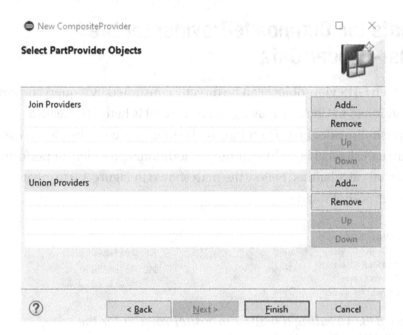

Figure 3-9. *Selecting PartProviders and defining the default node for the ZCPEXT01 CompositeProvider*

The Join Providers section requires you to provide at least two PartProviders. The Union Providers section can be used when we want to consume only a single PartProvider, so we could add the ZEXTORD01 Open ODS View to this section. Optionally we can go directly to the CompositeProvider editor without providing the InfoProviders information. I skipped the step of providing the provider information and clicked the Finish button.

I used the default settings for the CompositeProvider, so on the General tab I did not apply any changes and switched to the Scenario tab. Since I didn't specify any providers, the Scenario tab shows just a default node, which is Union. To add the ZCPEXT01 Open ODS View, click the Add button, as in Figure 3-10.

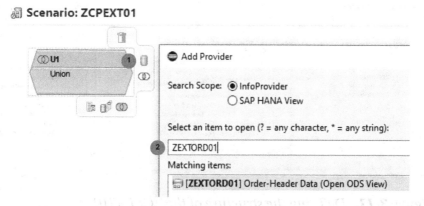

Figure 3-10. *Adding the ZEXTORD01 Open ODS View to the ZCPEXT01 CompositeProvider*

After clicking the Add button on the Union node, the Add Provider window opens. There are two Search Scope options: InfoProvider and SAP HANA View. Since we are looking for the Open ODS View, the InfoProvider should be selected for the Search Scope setting. Then in the search dialog, enter the name of the InfoProvider object. As shown in Figure 3-10, I entered the Open ODS View technical name and then selected the target object. When we add the source InfoProvider object to the CompositeProvider, we will be able to define the CompositeProvider structure based on the available source fields. In our scenario, we need to simply add all the fields from the source to the target. This can be done by selecting all the fields (click the first field, and then press the Shift key and select the last field) and dragging them to the Target section. Optionally, we can right-click the Open ODS View icon and select the Create Assignments option, as shown in Figure 3-11.

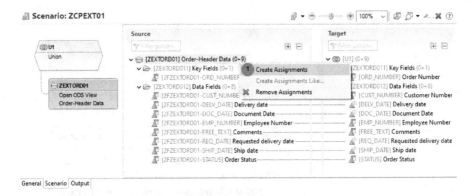

Figure 3-11. *Defining the structure of the ZCPEXT01 CompositeProvider*

When using the Create Assignments option, all fields will be automatically added to the output of the CompositeProvider. Names and descriptions will be also populated accordingly to the source fields.

Note   Unique field names for the CompositeProviders are generated automatically following this pattern: 4Z<CompositeProvider Name>-<Field Name>. The System-Wide Unique Name setting cannot be modified.

As shown in Figure 3-11, nine fields were added to the Target section of the ZCPEXT01 CompositeProvider. After defining the desired output structure of the CompositeProvider, activate it.

Important   When activating the CompositeProvider on top of the Open ODS View, you might see a CalcIndex-related issue. To fix the activation error, you need to run the ABAP program, which creates a column view for the Open ODS View.

As mentioned, for the given scenario, the activation of the
CompositeProvider might return a CalcIndex error. The error description
will look as follows:

```
'XXX::SAPABAP1:OBW:BIA:ZEXTORD01:EXTRACTION (t -1)'"
  Could not activate object 'ZCPEXT01'
  Creation of column view for ZCPEXT01 failed
  EC:2048"column store error: fail to create scenario: [2007]
Index does not exist;Failed to get
```

To fix this issue, you need to go to the SAP GUI and run the SE38 tcode.
Then run the program RSDDB_LOGINDEX_CREATE (Figure 3-12).

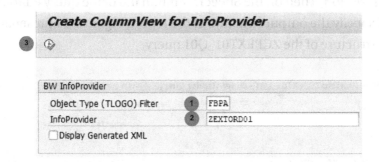

Figure 3-12. *Generating a ColumnView with the RSDDB_*
LOGINDEX_CREATE program

In that program, set FBPA (1) as the object type and provide the name
of your InfoProvider (2). Once you run the program (3) and the Column
View is successfully activated, go back to the CompositeProvider and try to
activate it again. The error should not appear anymore.

Create the Query for the Order-Header Data

The last step to fulfill the requirements described in Case Study 1 is to
create a query that users will consume in front-end tools to access data
from the external ORDER_HEADER table. The query will be created on

top of the CompositeProvider ZCPEXT01. Follow the steps shown in
Figure 3-13 to create a new query on CompositeProvider.

Figure 3-13. *Creating a new query on the ZCPEXT01*
CompositeProvider

When creating a new query, the system will ask for a technical name
and description. Then on the Sheet Definition tab of the query editor, we
should specify the output structure of the report. Figure 3-14 presents the
output structure of the ZCPEXT01_Q01 query.

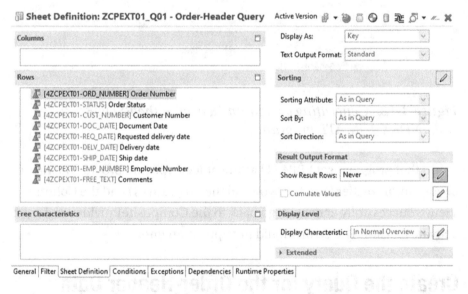

Figure 3-14. *Definition of the ZCPEXT01_Q01 query*

The fields available in the underlying CompositeProvider can be added to the output of the query by right-clicking one of the blank sections (Columns, Rows, or Free Characteristics) available on the Sheet Definition tab. As shown in Figure 3-14, all CompositeProvider fields have been added to the Rows section of the query. This means that when running the query in the front-end tool, all the fields will be added to the output of the report by default. At this point, no additional settings are required, so we can simply save the query. To preview the output of the query, I will use the Analysis for Microsoft Excel tool. Figure 3-15 shows the final output of the ZCPEXT01_Q01 query.

Order Number	Order Status	Customer Number	Document Date	Requested delivery date	Delivery date
0000000001	001	0100000010	17.08.2004	27.08.2004	26.08.2004
0000000002	001	0100000011	19.08.2004	28.08.2004	31.08.2004
0000000003	001	0100000011	20.08.2004	26.08.2004	31.08.2004
0000000004	001	0100000013	20.08.2004	30.08.2004	31.08.2004
0000000005	001	0100000013	21.08.2004	29.08.2004	03.09.2004
0000000006	001	0100000013	27.08.2004	04.09.2004	05.09.2004
0000000007	001	0100000010	28.08.2004	06.09.2004	08.09.2004

Figure 3-15. *Output of the ZCPEXT01_Q01 query in Analysis for Microsoft Excel*

Figure 3-15 shows the content of the first six characteristics available in the ZCPEXT01_Q01 query. The structure of the final report corresponds to the structure of the source table; hence, the requirement specified in Case Study 1 has been fulfilled. The same approach can be followed if the scenario required using a source virtual table instead of a persistent table.

Publish HANA Views Through BW/4HANA

CASE STUDY 2

After providing the query ZCPEXT01_Q01 to the business users, they validated the output and came back with two additional requirements.

Requirement 1: The first requirement is to add a column displaying text for order statuses. To get the status name, it is required to use an additional ORDER_STATUS table. This dimension table helps to look up a status description for given order status IDs. In Table 3-3, you will find details of the ORDER_STATUS table structure.

Table 3-3. *Structure of the ORDER_STATUS Table*

Column Name	Key	Data Type	Description
STATUS_ID	X	VARCHAR(3)	Status ID
STATUS_DESC		VARCHAR(30)	Status name
LANGU		VARCHAR(2)	Language

Table ORDER_STATUS consists of three columns where STATUS_ID is a primary key.

Requirement 2: A business user requested to add a new column to the report that will calculate the difference between the Delivery Date and Requested Delivery values in days.

Create the Calculation View for the Order-Header Data

As per Requirement 1 from Case Study 2, we need to combine two HANA tables. This can be achieved by leveraging the calculation view capabilities. The general approach that I will follow for this case study is illustrated in Figure 2-5 of Chapter 2. Unlike in Figure 2-5, the calculation view will query data only from persistent HANA tables (virtual tables will not be used). Figure 3-16 shows the objects that I will be using to fulfill the requirements from Case Study 2.

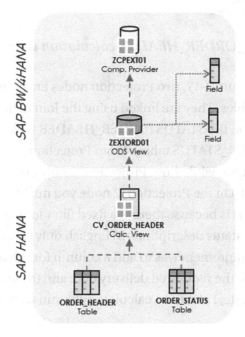

Figure 3-16. *Publishing HANA views through BW/4HANA (Case Study 2)*

Two HANA tables will be joined on the calculation view level. Then the existing Open ODS View object will be updated by changing the underlying data source and adding new fields.

To join the ORDER_HEADER and ORDER_STATUS tables, I created the CV_ORDER_HEADER calculation view (see Figure 3-17).

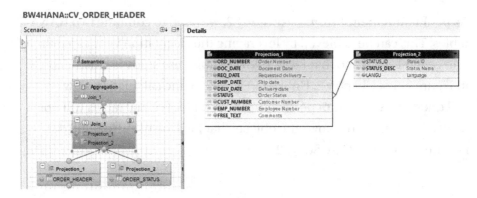

Figure 3-17. *CV_ORDER_HEADER calculation view definition*

As shown in Figure 3-17, two Projection nodes are pointing to the required HANA tables. They are linked using the Join node. Join is performed based on the STATUS (ORDER_HEADER table) and STATUS_ ID columns (ORDER_STATUS table). From Projection_1, all fields are mapped to the output, while from Projection_2 only the STATUS_DESC column is selected. On the Projection_2 node you might notice the filter icon displayed. This is because there is a fixed filter for the Language column to display status descriptions in English only (LANGU = 'E').

The second requirement was to add a column for calculating the difference between the requested delivery date and the actual delivery date. In the Join node, I created a calculated column with the following SQL syntax:

```
CASE WHEN "STATUS_DESC" = 'Delivered'
THEN  days_between("REQ_DATE", "DELV_DATE") END
```

This formula calculates the number of days between the requested delivery date (REQ_DATE) and the delivery date (DELV_DATE) for all

116

records with an order status value equal to Delivered. The previous SQL formula is used in the Expression Editor of the CM_DELV_DATE_DIFF calculated column (Figure 3-18).

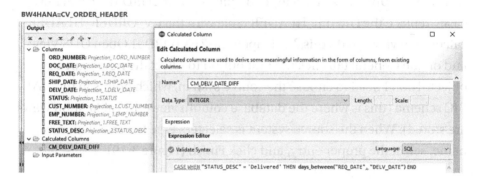

Figure 3-18. *CM_DELV_DATE_DIFF calculated column definition*

The calculated column CM_DELV_DATE_DIFF is of the INTEGER data type. The language for the Expression Editor is set to SQL, as the formula is written in SQL. After providing the expression, it is worth checking whether the syntax has any errors by clicking the Validate Syntax button. If the formula is correct, after clicking this button you should see a "Valid Expression" message.

Note   The Expression Editor does not recognize all SQL functions; hence, it might highlight the syntax as an error even though it is valid. This refers to SQL functions that are not available in the Functions list of the Expression Editor. Please also be aware that not all SQL functions can be used in graphical views.

Change the Source Object for the Order-Header Open ODS View

By using the Open ODS View functionality, for ZEXTORD01 we can now easily replace the ORDER_HEADER table with the CV_ORDER_HEADER calculation view. To do this, I will open the ZEXTORD01 Open ODS View and on the General tab click the Edit button to select the new source object. Then I need to choose the source system, which points to the _SYS_ BIC schema (this is where the database column views for calculation views are stored). When the source system is selected, type the calculation view name, select the proper entry, and click Finish (Figure 3-19).

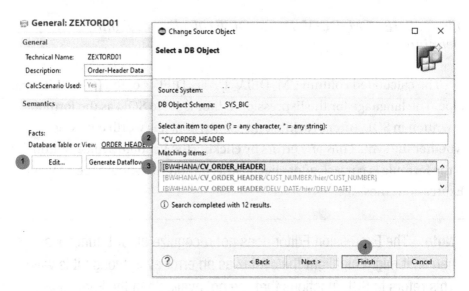

Figure 3-19. *Changing the source object for the ZEXTORD01 Open ODS View*

Once the source object is replaced, the Semantics section of the General tab should be updated with the new object name. In the Facts tab, the fields that were not yet added to the output will be highlighted in gray, as in Figure 3-20.

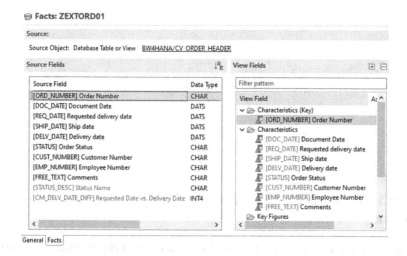

Figure 3-20. *Open ODS View for the CV_ORDER_HEADER View, Facts tab*

On the Facts tab I need to add two new fields that were requested by the user: Status Name and Requested Date vs. Delivery Date (Days). Status Name is an attribute; hence, it should go under the Characteristics folder, while Requested Date vs. Delivery Date (Days) is a measure, so it should be dragged under Key Figures folder. When the target structure of the Open ODS View is defined, I can activate the Open ODS View.

Update the CompositeProvider for the Order-Header Data

There are two remaining objects that require a structure update: the ZCPEXT01 CompositeProvider object and the ZCPEXT01_Q01 Query object. Since I added two new fields to the ZEXTORD01 Open ODS View, they should already be available in the Source section of the ZCPEXT01 CompositeProvider (Figure 3-21).

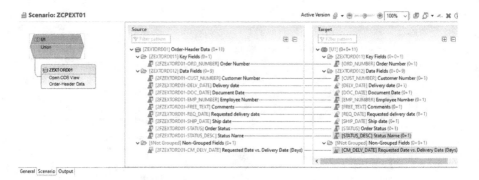

Figure 3-21. *Adding new fields to the ZCPEXT01 CompositeProvider structure*

As shown in Figure 3-21, new ODS fields (Status Name and Requested Date vs. Delivery Date (Days)) are available in the Source section. To add them to the final structure, drag and drop them from the Source section to the Target section. Then activate the CompositeProvider.

Note   If you see a "column view" error during CompositeProvider activation, run again the RSDDB_LOGINDEX_CREATE program for the underlying Open ODS View to create a column view (see Figure 3-12).

Update the Query for the Order-Header Data

The final step for Case Study 2 is to include new fields in the ZCPEXT01_Q01 query. Figure 3-22 presents the final definition of the ZCPEXT01_Q01 query.

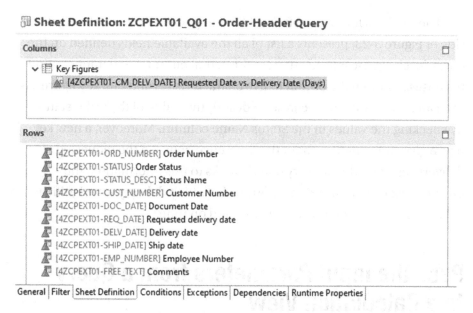

***Figure 3-22.** Adding new fields to the ZCPEXT01_Q01 query definition*

The Status Name characteristic is added to the Rows section, while the Requested Date vs. Delivery Date (Days) key figure is placed in the Columns section. After running the query, by default all fields will be displayed in the output. The user can adjust the report structure according to the needs. Figure 3-23 displays the updated output of the ZCPEXT01_Q01 query.

Order Number	Order Status	Status Name	Requested delivery date	Delivery date	Requested Date vs. Delivery Date (Days)
0000000001	001	Delivered	27.08.2004	26.08.2004	-1
0000000002	001	Delivered	28.08.2004	31.08.2004	3
0000000003	001	Delivered	26.08.2004	31.08.2004	5
0000000004	001	Delivered	30.08.2004	31.08.2004	1
0000000005	001	Delivered	29.08.2004	03.09.2004	5
0000000006	001	Delivered	04.09.2004	05.09.2004	1
0000000007	001	Delivered	06.09.2004	08.09.2004	2
0000000008	001	Delivered	06.09.2004	08.09.2004	2
0000000009	001	Delivered	11.09.2004	14.09.2004	3
0000000010	001	Delivered	13.09.2004	11.09.2004	-2
0000000011	001	Delivered	15.09.2004	20.09.2004	5
0000000012	001	Delivered	17.09.2004	22.09.2004	5
0000000013	001	Delivered	18.09.2004	21.09.2004	3
0000000014	002	In Process	18.09.2004	#	0
0000000015	002	In Process	17.09.2004	#	0
0000000016	002	In Process	17.09.2004	#	0

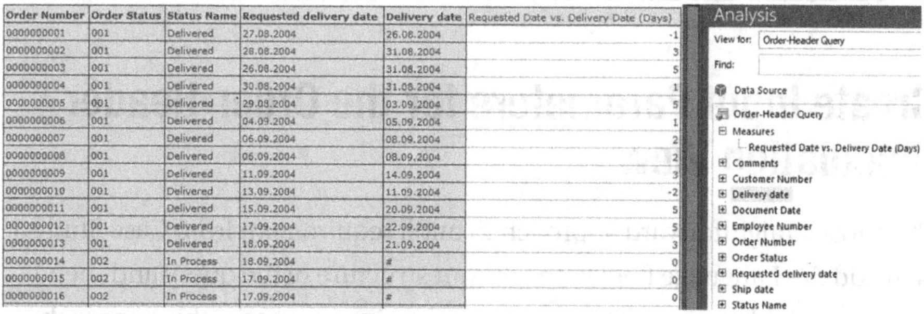

***Figure 3-23.** New fields of the ZCPEXT01_Q01 query in Analysis for Microsoft Excel*

The Analysis for Microsoft Excel Design panel, shown on the right side of Figure 3-23, presents a list of all the available fields defined on the query level. On the left side there is the actual output. For demonstration purposes, I limited the output to five characteristics and one key figure. As you can see, now the user can see a descriptive value of the order status by checking the values in the Status Name column. Moreover, a new key figure gives information about the difference between the requested delivery date and the delivery date. Thanks to this information, the business user can easily identify orders for which delivery was significantly delayed, as well as identify those delivered on time.

Pass the Input Parameters from a Query to a Calculation View

CASE STUDY 3

Business users requested the ability to select the display language for status names before running the report. When opening the report, the user should be prompted to choose a Language Variable value. According to the entered value, in the output of the report, the Status Name column should display the text in the proper language.

Create Input Parameters for the Order-Header Calculation View

The most straightforward approach to fulfill requirement from Case Study 3 is to add the Language field to the output structure of the query and then create a variable on top of that field. For the given scenario, this approach is sufficient, because the underlying calculation view is simple, and it does not process huge data volumes and complex logic with many tables; hence, performance will not be impacted. Nevertheless, there might be a scenario when the source calculation view is much more complex and needs to handle operations on very big tables. In such a case, the HANA engine might not be able to push down the filter to the data foundation level of the view. This may significantly impact the performance.

To ensure that the value entered on the selection screen is pushed down to the table level, I will create an input parameter on the calculation view level and then map it to the query variable. Let's now open the CV_ORDER_HEADER calculation view and select the Projection node, which points to the ORDER_STATUS table. To create a new input parameter, go to the Output section, right-click the Input Parameters folder, and select New (Figure 3-24).

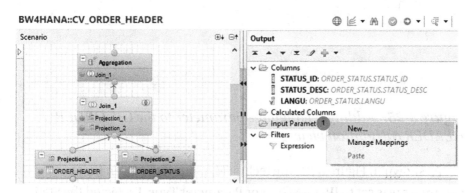

Figure 3-24. Adding a Language parameter to the CV_ORDER_HEADER calculation view

When adding a new input parameter, the system will open the New Input Parameter window. Here we can configure the properties of the parameter. Figure 3-25 shows the properties of the Language input parameter.

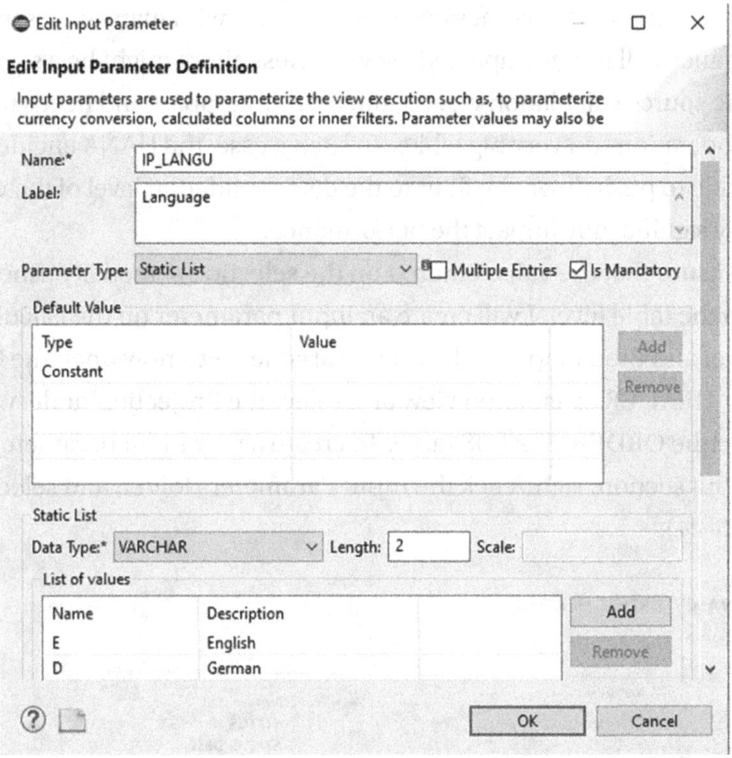

Figure 3-25. *Adding a Language parameter to the CV_ORDER_*
HEADER calculation view

As shown in Figure 3-25, the technical name of the given input parameter was set to IP_LANGU. For Parameter Type, I selected the Static List option. This means that for the Parameter value's help, I need to define a list of fixed values. This list is specified in the "List of values" section. In the given example, I entered two values into the list: E for English and D for German. The Is Mandatory check box indicates that the input parameter's value needs to be provided to be able to run the report. The data type was set to VARCHAR with a length of 2. This type corresponds to the source data type of the Language column. Now we need to link the input parameter with the LANGU column filter. Right-click the LANGU column and select Edit Filter or Apply Filter (depending on whether filter was previously

applied on that column or not). Instead of filtering the LANGU column
with the Fixed value, change the filter value type to Input Parameters. Then
select the IP_LANGU parameter as a filter value (Figure 3-26).

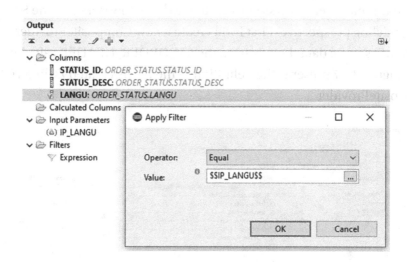

Figure 3-26. *Applying the IP_LANGU parameter as a column filter
in the CV_ORDER_HEADER calculation view*

IP_LANGU is a single-value input parameter, so when filtering the
LANGU column, we should use an Equal value for the filter operator. To
validate the input parameter, activate your view and execute the calculation
view. When previewing the view, you should be prompted with a
parameters screen. The output of the view should display the Status Name
text values according to the language selected for the input parameter.

Note   Open ODS Views do not support calculation views with
input parameters. After adding the mandatory input parameters to
the calculation view, it cannot be consumed by the Open ODS View
anymore. This means that previously created BW/4HANA objects
(Open ODS View, Composite Provider, and Query) will throw an error
when trying to preview the data.

Create the CompositeProvider for the Order-Header Data with Input Parameters

If the input parameter works as expected, we can now switch to the SAP BW modeling perspective. First I will create a new CompositeProvider, which will source data directly from the CV_ORDER_HEADER calculation view. Figure 3-27 presents the definition of the newly created ZCPEXT02 CompositeProvider.

Figure 3-27. *Defining the structure of the ZCPEXT02 CompositeProvider*

Mapping between the source and target fields looks almost the same as in the CompositeProvider ZCPEXT01 (presented in Figure 3-21). You might notice that there is one more field available in the ZCPEXT02 CompositeProvider structure. This is the field representing the HANA input parameter (IP_LANGU), which was created in the CV_ORDER_HEADER calculation view. This Input Parameter field can be later used as a reference for a variable at the query level. When the CompositeProvider is active, we can then create a new query (ZCPEXT02_Q01) on top of it.

Create the Query for the Order-Header Data with Input Parameters

The output structure (on the Sheet Definition tab) of the ZCPEXT02_Q01 query will be the same as in the previous scenario (see Figure 3-22 for reference). The mapping between the calculation view's input parameter and query's variable will be defined on the Filter tab of the query.

Note   You should not add input parameter fields to any section within the Sheet Definition tab because when running the query, you would get an error. Input parameter fields are not permitted for navigation; they should be used only for filtering.

As a first step, I will add the Language input parameter to the Filter: Fixed Values section. To do so, right-click the Filter: Fixed Values area and select the Add Characteristic option. Then browse for the input parameter name, select it, and click the OK button (Figure 3-28).

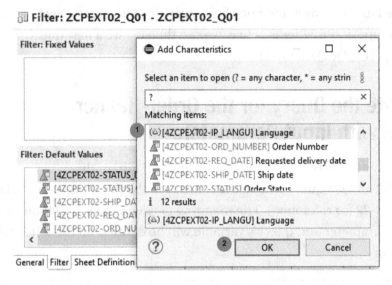

Figure 3-28. *Adding the input parameter field to the Filter section of the ZCPEXT02_Q01 query*

Once the input parameter is added to the Filter section, we need to create a Language query variable. Before doing that, copy to the clipboard the technical name of the input parameter (in my case it is 4ZCPEXT02-IP_LANGU). Then go to the Project Explorer and select New ➤ Variable (see Figure 3-29).

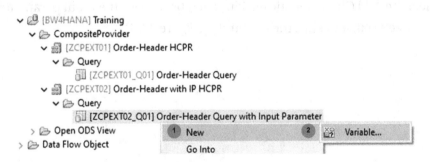

Figure 3-29. *Adding a new query variable*

When creating a new variable, the system will open the New Variable editor window. Here you need to provide a definition of the variable (Figure 3-30).

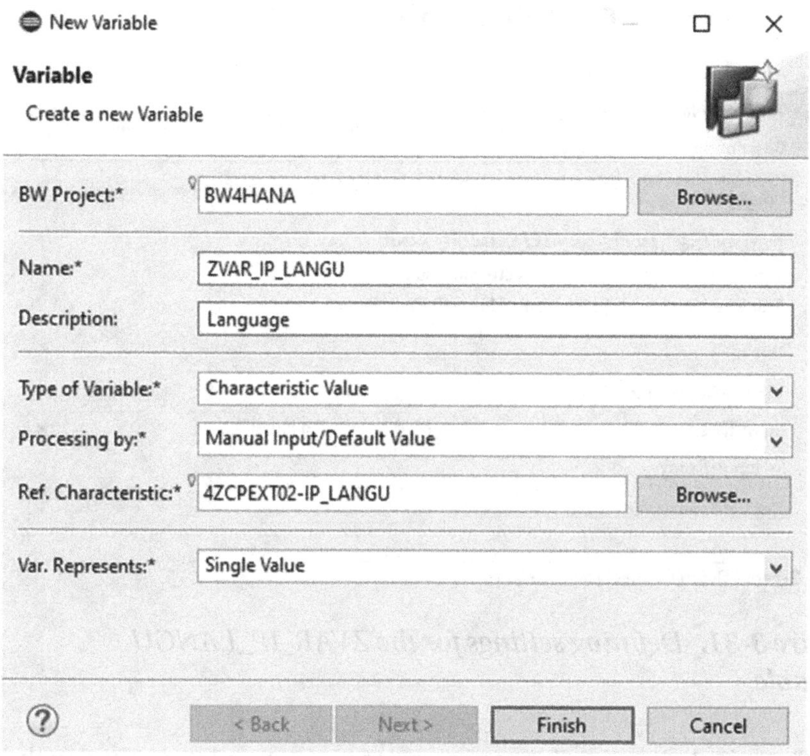

Figure 3-30 *Creating the ZVAR_IP_LANGU query variable*

The technical name of the Input Parameter field, which we copied to the clipboard, should now be pasted to the Ref. Characteristic field. The Browse option provides functionality to search for InfoObjects only; hence, when using the field-based approach, we need to enter the field technical names manually. The variable properties should match the settings of the HANA input parameter, so in our case we need to make sure that the variable represents a Single Value type. After validating the general variable properties, click the Finish button to close the wizard and proceed with the variable's detailed settings (Figure 3-31).

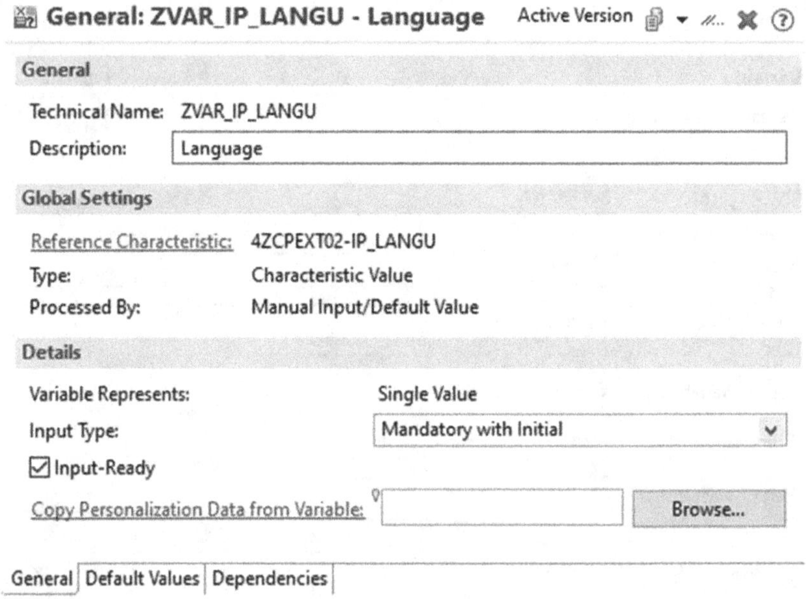

General: ZVAR_IP_LANGU - Language   Active Version

General

Technical Name: ZVAR_IP_LANGU

Description: Language

Global Settings

Reference Characteristic: 4ZCPEXT02-IP_LANGU

Type: Characteristic Value

Processed By: Manual Input/Default Value

Details

Variable Represents: Single Value

Input Type: Mandatory with Initial

☑ Input-Ready

Copy Personalization Data from Variable: Browse...

General | Default Values | Dependencies

Figure 3-31. *Defining settings for the ZVAR_IP_LANGU variable*

The calculation view input parameter is of a mandatory type, so the same setting should be applied for the query variable's input type. In addition, on the Default Values tab we can set the default value for the Language variable. When the configuration is completed, save the variable and go back to the Query Filter definition. Now we can map the calculation view parameter to the query variable. Right-click the technical name of the input parameter and choose the Restrict option (Figure 3-32).

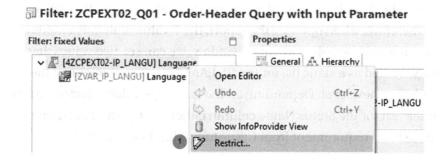

Figure 3-32. *Mapping the 4ZCPEXT02-IP_LANGU input parameter field to the query variable*

In the filter editor, select the proper variable (in my scenario it will be ZVAR_IP_LANGU) and add it to the Filter Definition section. Once you confirm the variable selection, you will see the variable in the Filter: Fixed Values section (as shown in Figure 3-32). Now we can save the query and run it to check the results. When opening the ZCPEXT02_Q01 query in Analysis for Microsoft Excel, the selection screen opens (Figure 3-33).

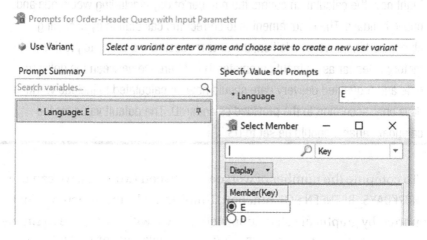

Figure 3-33. *Analysis for Microsoft Excel prompting for the ZCPEXT02_Q01 query*

I set the default value for the Language variable (ZVAR_IP_LANGU) to E; therefore, when opening the report, the E value is already entered. When opening the Select Member window, we can see two values that were specified as a static list for the IP_LANGU input parameter at the calculation view level. Depending on the Language value selected, the user will see text for the Status Name column either in English or in German. The business requirement from Case Study 3 has been fulfilled.

Pass Input Parameters from the Query to the Table Function

CASE STUDY 4

The business user realized that the current calculation of the difference between the delivery date and the requested delivery date is not very precise. Right now the calculation counts the number of days including weekends and public holidays. The requirement is to correct the calculation by excluding all nonworking days. In addition, the user requested the ability to provide a factory calendar as an input parameter. The difference between the delivery date and requested delivery date should now be calculated to include working days only, according to the provided calendar ID. The default value for the calendar variable should be set to US.

To compute the number of workdays between two dates, we can use the WORKDAYS_BETWEEN SQL function. Unfortunately, this function is not supported by graphical calculation views, so we will not be able to simply adjust the existing calculation. To utilize the WORKDAYS_BETWEEN function, we need to create a table function first. There are two approaches that I cover for the given scenario.

The first approach is to convert the entire calculation view (CV_ORDER_HEADER) logic into a SQL script. All the joins and calculations need to be manually converted into the SQL code and included in the table function definition (Figure 3-34).

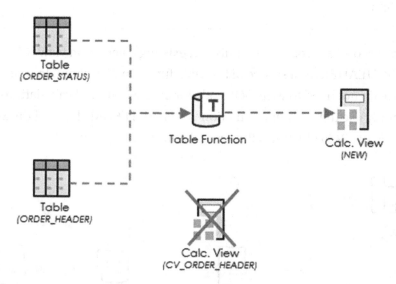

Figure 3-34. *Replacing the existing calculation view with the table function*

As shown in Figure 3-34, the table function consumes source tables directly. For the considered scenario, it would be easy to translate the logic from a graphical view into the SQL script. There are just two tables to be joined; hence, this approach might be preferable. Moreover, the existing calculation view would not be needed anymore and could be removed. Therefore, there would be only two objects to be maintained on the HANA native side: the table function and the calculation view.

Note   Table functions cannot be consumed directly by CompositeProviders, so there is a need to create a calculation view as an intermediate layer between a CompositeProvider and a table function.

The second approach is to utilize an existing calculation view (CV_ ORDER_HEADER) as a source of the table function SQL script. In that case, we do not need to write SQL code for all the joins and calculations, but simply use the current calculation view in the FROM clause of the SQL script. Figure 3-35 illustrates the second approach.

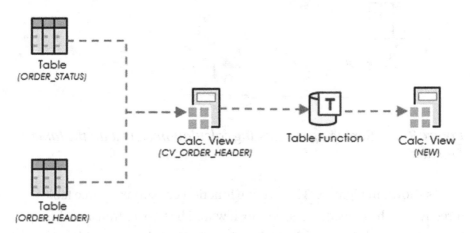

Figure 3-35. *Utilizing the existing calculation view in the table function*

Although the second approach is a bit faster to implement, I find the first one better from a maintenance perspective. In the approach depicted in Figure 3-35, there are three HANA modeling objects. On the other hand, if the underlying calculation view is complex and includes dozens of tables and calculations, the second approach could be the preferable one.

Despite that for the given scenario the first approach is more suitable, I will demonstrate how to fulfill the requirement from Case Study 4 using the second approach (Figure 3-35). This is because with this approach I will also have an opportunity to show how we can pass input parameter values from the table function to the underlying calculation view.

Prepare the SQL Query for the Order-Header Data

To start working on the table function, let's switch to the SAP development perspective. As a first step, we need to prepare the SELECT statement on top of the CV_ORDER_HEADER calculation view. Instead of writing SQL code manually from scratch, we can automatically generate the SELECT statement out of the calculation view and use it as a reference for further enhancements. From the Repositories explorer tree, find the desired calculation view that will be used as the reference, right-click it, and choose the Generate Select SQL option as in Figure 3-36.

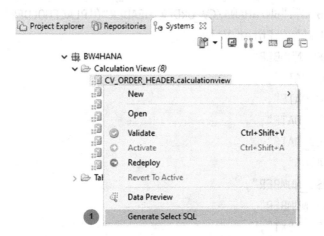

Figure 3-36. *Generating the SELECT SQL code from the calculation view*

135

After generating the SELECT SQL code from CV_ORDER_HEADER, Eclipse will open a new SQL console tab with the generated SELECT statement. A script generated out of CV_ORDER_HEADER has the following syntax:

```
SELECT
        "ORD_NUMBER",
        "DOC_DATE",
        "REQ_DATE",
        "SHIP_DATE",
        "DELV_DATE",
        "STATUS",
        "CUST_NUMBER",
        "EMP_NUMBER",
        "FREE_TEXT",
        "STATUS_DESC",
        sum("CM_DELV_DATE_DIFF") AS "CM_DELV_DATE_DIFF"
FROM "_SYS_BIC"."BW/4HANA/CV_ORDER_HEADER"('PLACEHOLDER' =
('$$IP_LANGU$$','<Enter Value>'))
GROUP BY "ORD_NUMBER",
        "DOC_DATE",
        "REQ_DATE",
        "SHIP_DATE",
        "DELV_DATE",
        "STATUS",
        "CUST_NUMBER",
        "EMP_NUMBER",
        "FREE_TEXT",
        "STATUS_DESC"
```

As you might notice, the generated code includes a placeholder for the Language input parameter, which also needs to be maintained when creating a table function. In addition, to be able to pass the value from the table function input parameter to the graphical calculation view parameter, we need to apply specific syntax, which I will also explain later.

Let's now focus on adjusting our SQL query to fulfill the requirements from Case Study 4. To be able to preview results in the SQL console from the generated query, we need to pass a valid value to the IP_LANGU input parameter. Temporarily I will fix the placeholder value as E. The syntax for the placeholder now looks as follows:

```
('PLACEHOLDER' = ('$$IP_LANGU$$','E'))
```

Now I want to create a new calculation to compute the number of working days between the delivery date and requested delivery date. As mentioned, I will use the WORKDAYS_BETWEEN function.

Note   To use the WORKDAYS_BETWEEN function, table TFACS must be available in any HANA database schemas. TFACS is a standard SAP table, which contains information about working and nonworking days for each year and calendar type.

The syntax for the WORKDAYS_BETWEEN function looks as follows:

```
WORKDAYS_BETWEEN(<calendar_id>, <start_date>, <end_date>,
<schema_name>)
```

Here you will find the meaning of the syntax elements:

- <calendar_id>: This specifies the ID for the factory calendar, which will be used as a reference for excluding weekends and public holidays from the computation. As per the requirements (Case Study 4) this value should be dynamically defined based on user input.

- `<start_date>`: This represents the start date for calculating the difference in working days.
- `<end_date>`: This represents the end date for calculating difference in working days.
- `<schema_name>`: This specifies the schema name in which the TFACS table is stored.

To test the function in the SQL console, I will temporarily set the value for `<calendar_id>` to US. For `<start_date>` I will use the Requested Delivery Date column, and for `<end_date>` I will use Delivery Date. In my HANA system, the TFACS table is stored in the SAPABAP1 schema; hence, in place of `<schema_name>`, I will input the SAPABAP1 value. The syntax for calculating days between the delivery date and requested delivery date will look as follows:

```
WORKDAYS_BETWEEN('US',"REQ_DATE","DELV_DATE",'SAPABAP1')
```

This function will later be adjusted to manage dynamic input for the factory calendar parameter. In Figure 3-37 you will find the results of the previous calculation (column CM_DELV_DATE_DIFF_WD).

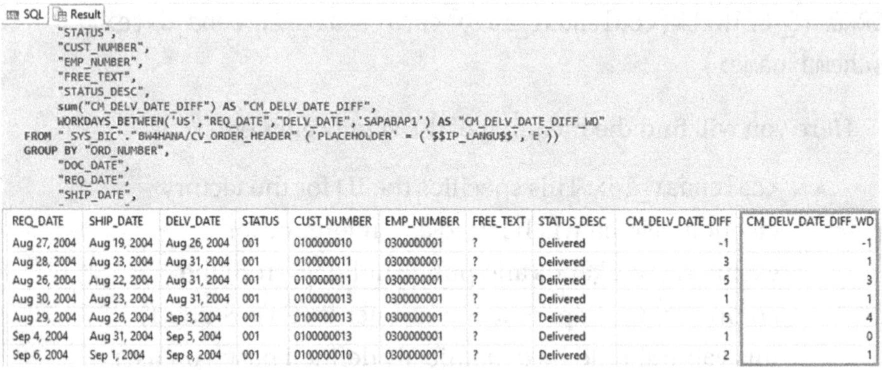


```
       "STATUS",
       "CUST_NUMBER",
       "EMP_NUMBER",
       "FREE_TEXT",
       "STATUS_DESC",
       sum("CM_DELV_DATE_DIFF") AS "CM_DELV_DATE_DIFF",
       WORKDAYS_BETWEEN('US',"REQ_DATE","DELV_DATE",'SAPABAP1') AS "CM_DELV_DATE_DIFF_WD"
  FROM "_SYS_BIC"."BW4HANA/CV_ORDER_HEADER" ('PLACEHOLDER' = ('$$IP_LANGU$$','E'))
  GROUP BY "ORD_NUMBER",
       "DOC_DATE",
       "REQ_DATE",
       "SHIP_DATE",
```

REQ_DATE	SHIP_DATE	DELV_DATE	STATUS	CUST_NUMBER	EMP_NUMBER	FREE_TEXT	STATUS_DESC	CM_DELV_DATE_DIFF	CM_DELV_DATE_DIFF_WD
Aug 27, 2004	Aug 19, 2004	Aug 26, 2004	001	0100000010	0300000001	?	Delivered	-1	-1
Aug 28, 2004	Aug 23, 2004	Aug 31, 2004	001	0100000011	0300000001	?	Delivered	3	1
Aug 26, 2004	Aug 22, 2004	Aug 31, 2004	001	0100000011	0300000001	?	Delivered	5	3
Aug 30, 2004	Aug 23, 2004	Aug 31, 2004	001	0100000013	0300000001	?	Delivered	1	1
Aug 29, 2004	Aug 26, 2004	Sep 3, 2004	001	0100000013	0300000001	?	Delivered	5	4
Sep 4, 2004	Aug 31, 2004	Sep 5, 2004	001	0100000013	0300000001	?	Delivered	1	0
Sep 6, 2004	Sep 1, 2004	Sep 8, 2004	001	0100000010	0300000001	?	Delivered	2	1

Figure 3-37. *Results of SQL query with WORKDAYS_BETWEEN calculation*

Figure 3-37 shows the result of the SQL query on top of the CV_ ORDER_HEADER view. In addition to columns being derived directly from the view, there is a calculated column with the CM_DELV_DATE_DIFF_ WD alias. This calculated column uses the WORKDAYS_BETWEEN function to calculate the difference between the delivery date and the requested delivery date. When you compare the results of the new calculation (CM_DELV_DATE_DIFF_WD) with the calculation derived from the view (CM_DELV_DATE_DIFF), you will notice that the values in the former one are in most cases lower than for the latter one. The column CM_ DELV_DATE_DIFF_WD calculates the result based on the WORKDAYS_BETWEEN function, while the column CM_DELV_DATE_DIFF computes the number of days based on the DAYS_BETWEEN function. This means that the new calculation excludes nonworking days, so if between two dates there will be any public holiday or weekend, these days will not be included when counting the total number of days. This is why for some order entries, the CM_DELV_DATE_DIFF_WD column shows lower numbers compared to the CM_DELV_DATE_DIFF column.

Create the Table Function for the Order-Header Data

After validating the query and checking its results, we can start creating a new table function. Follow the steps described in the section "Table Functions" of Chapter 1 to open the table function editor. I divided the table function definition into the three sections highlighted in Figure 3-38. The numbers indicate the order for creating each section of the table function definition.

```
Table Function
 1  FUNCTION "_SYS_BIC"."BW4HANA::TF_ORDER_HEADER" ( IP_LANGU VARCHAR(2), IP_CALENDAR VARCHAR(2) )
 2
 3      RETURNS TABLE
 4      (
 5          ORD_NUMBER VARCHAR(10),
 6          DOC_DATE DATE,
 7          REQ_DATE DATE,
 8          SHIP_DATE DATE,
 9          DELV_DATE DATE,
10          STATUS VARCHAR(3),
11          CUST_NUMBER VARCHAR(10),
12          EMP_NUMBER VARCHAR(10),
13          FREE_TEXT VARCHAR(100),
14          STATUS_DESC VARCHAR(30),
15          CM_DELV_DATE_DIFF_WD INTEGER
16      )
17      LANGUAGE SQLSCRIPT
18      SQL SECURITY INVOKER AS
19
20  BEGIN
21
22      RETURN
23
24          SELECT
25              "ORD_NUMBER",
26              "DOC_DATE",
27              "REQ_DATE",
28              "SHIP_DATE",
29              "DELV_DATE",
30              "STATUS",
31              "CUST_NUMBER",
32              "EMP_NUMBER",
33              "FREE_TEXT",
34              "STATUS_DESC",
35                  WORKDAYS_BETWEEN( :IP_CALENDAR, "REQ_DATE", "DELV_DATE", 'SAPABAP1')
36              AS "CM_DELV_DATE_DIFF_WD"
37          FROM "_SYS_BIC"."BW4HANA/CV_ORDER_HEADER"
38              (
39                  PLACEHOLDER."$$IP_LANGU$$"  => :IP_LANGU
40              )
41          ;
42
43  END;
```

Figure 3-38. *Definition of the TF_ORDER_HEADER table function*

1. In the first part of the code, I indicated the target
    schema name for the table function (_SYS_BIC)
    and defined two input parameters. The first one
    (IP_LANGU) will be used to pass the Language
    value into the CV_ORDER_HEADER calculation
    view input parameter. IP_CALENDAR is a new
    parameter requested by the user to determine the
    calendar type used as a reference for calculating

the difference between the delivery date and the
requested delivery date.

```
FUNCTION "_SYS_BIC"."BW/4HANA::TF_ORDER_HEADER"
( IP_LANGU VARCHAR(2), IP_CALENDAR VARCHAR(2) )
```

2. The actual query is surrounded by the BEGIN and
   END operators. The SELECT query that I defined
   in the SQL console (Figure 3-37) was copied into
   the table function definition. For the WORKDAYS_
   BETWEEN function, the previously fixed US calendar
   ID value has now been replaced with the dynamic
   IP_CALENDAR input parameter.

```
WORKDAYS_BETWEEN(:IP_CALENDAR, "REQ_DATE",
"DELV_DATE", 'SAPABAP1')
```

In addition, when applying the mapping between
the table function language input parameter and
the calculation view input parameter, the syntax for
the placeholder needs to be modified to make this
mapping work properly. Here is the valid syntax for
passing the table function input parameter value to
the calculation view input parameter:

```
( PLACEHOLDER."$$IP_LANGU$$"  => :IP_LANGU )
```

Note   In SQL, table function input parameters are called using a
colon (i.e., :IP_LANGU), while placeholders for calculation view
input parameters are surrounded by double quotes and double dollar
symbols (i.e., "$$IP_LANGU$$").

The final SELECT query looks like this:

```
SELECT
  "ORD_NUMBER",
  "DOC_DATE",
  "REQ_DATE",
  "SHIP_DATE",
  "DELV_DATE",
  "STATUS",
  "CUST_NUMBER",
  "EMP_NUMBER",
  "FREE_TEXT",
  "STATUS_DESC",
        WORKDAYS_BETWEEN( :IP_CALENDAR, "REQ_DATE",
"DELV_DATE", 'SAPABAP1')
  AS "CM_DELV_DATE_DIFF_WD"
FROM "_SYS_BIC"."BW/4HANA/CV_ORDER_HEADER"
        (
            PLACEHOLDER."$$IP_LANGU$$"  => :IP_LANGU
        )
```

3. I always define this section once I have the final
    SELECT query prepared. This is because in this
    section you need to provide data types for each
    column listed in the final SELECT query. Also,
    the column order needs to be preserved. As I
    mentioned in Chapter 1, this part is error-prone;
    hence, it is important to define data types according
    to the source column types. Here we could open the
    source calculation view definition in the graphical
    editor to check each output column data type and
    use the same types in the table function definition.

Another approach could be to get column data types by running the SQL query against the "_SYS_BI". "BIMC_PROPERTIES" metadata table. The following query returns the data types for all the output columns available in the CV_ORDER_ HEADER view:

```
SELECT COLUMN_NAME, COLUMN_SQL_TYPE
FROM "_SYS_BI"."BIMC_PROPERTIES"
WHERE CUBE_NAME = 'CV_ORDER_HEADER'
        AND DIMENSION_TYPE IS NOT NULL
```

The previous query will provide you with the list of columns and its data types. Figure 3-39 shows the output of the previous statement.

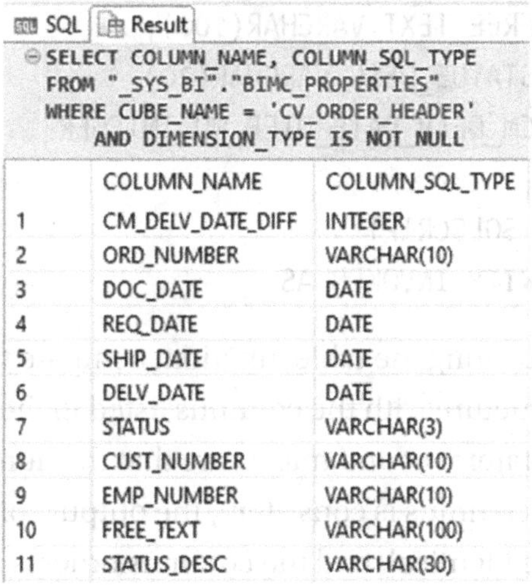

	COLUMN_NAME	COLUMN_SQL_TYPE
1	CM_DELV_DATE_DIFF	INTEGER
2	ORD_NUMBER	VARCHAR(10)
3	DOC_DATE	DATE
4	REQ_DATE	DATE
5	SHIP_DATE	DATE
6	DELV_DATE	DATE
7	STATUS	VARCHAR(3)
8	CUST_NUMBER	VARCHAR(10)
9	EMP_NUMBER	VARCHAR(10)
10	FREE_TEXT	VARCHAR(100)
11	STATUS_DESC	VARCHAR(30)

Figure 3-39. *Output of query for the CV_ORDER_HEADER calculation view properties*

You can then copy this list to the table function output definition. Then you will make sure that all data types are consistent with the source object structure. The following code defines the output structure of the TF_ORDER_HEADER table function:

```
RETURNS TABLE
(
        ORD_NUMBER VARCHAR(10),
        DOC_DATE DATE,
        REQ_DATE DATE,
        SHIP_DATE DATE,
        DELV_DATE DATE,
        STATUS VARCHAR(3),
        CUST_NUMBER VARCHAR(10),
        EMP_NUMBER VARCHAR(10),
        FREE_TEXT VARCHAR(100),
        STATUS_DESC VARCHAR(30),
        CM_DELV_DATE_DIFF_WD INTEGER
)
LANGUAGE SQLSCRIPT
SQL SECURITY INVOKER AS
```

Before activating the table function, compare the output structure with the columns listed in the SELECT statement and make sure that the number of output columns is consistent, the output column names are identical, and the columns order is preserved. After successful activation, you can query the TF to check if it returns the desired output. When running the SELECT statement, remember to provide the input parameter values (unless default input parameter values were defined in TF definition). The

following code queries data from the TF_ORDER_
HEADER table function:

```
SELECT * FROM "_SYS_BIC"."BW/4HANA::TF_ORDER_HEADER" (
'E', 'US' )
```

Figure 3-40 shows the output of this query.

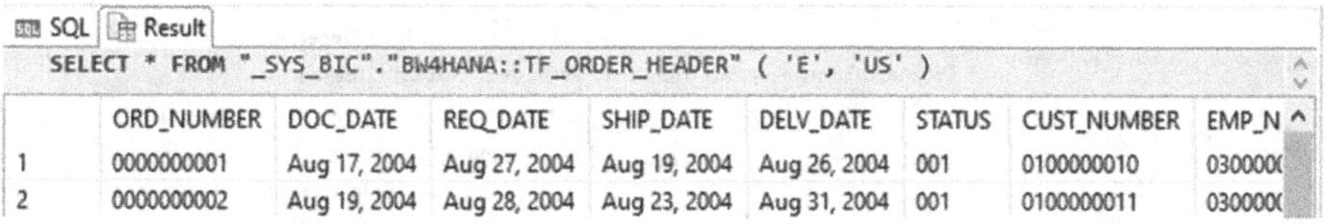

Figure 3-40. *Output of the query for the TF_ORDER_HEADER table function*

As shown in Figure 3-40, if we want to pass input
parameter values to the table function, we need to
specify values as a comma-separated list inside the
parentheses. Be aware that these input parameters are
the single-value type, so you cannot pass more than
one value for each parameter. Nevertheless, it is also
possible to maintain multiple-value input parameters,
but that requires additional coding within the table
function.

Create the Calculation View on Top of the Table Function

Next we need to create a calculation view on top of the TF_ORDER_HEADER
table function. I created a new calculation view of a CUBE type named CV_
ORDER_HEADER_TF. In this step, the important part will be to manage
the input parameter mapping properly. After adding the table function as a
data source of the calculation view, in the Semantics node we can manage

145

this mapping. To map the table function input parameter to the target parameter of the final calculation view, click the Semantics node and then go to the Parameters/Variables tab. After that, click the arrow symbol next to the input parameter's Manage Mapping button and select the Data Sources option (Figure 3-41).

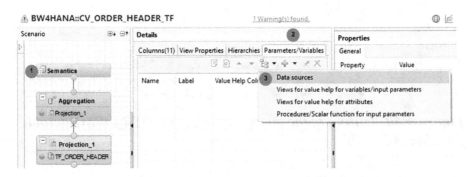

Figure 3-41. *Opening the window for input parameters mapping*

The Data Sources button opens a new window for managing the parameter mappings between the source and the target. Here we have an option to automatically create input parameters according to the parameters available in the underlying table function. By clicking the Auto Map By Name button (Figure 3-42), all input parameters will be automatically re-created and mapped to the source parameters. Figure 3-42 displays the parameters mapping between the TF_ORDER_HEADER table function and the CV_ORDER_HEADER_TF calculation view.

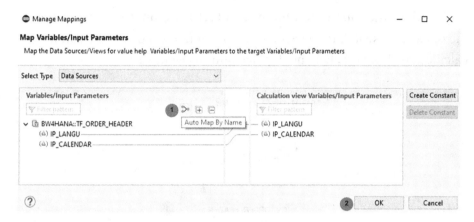

Figure 3-42. *Managing the input parameters mapping for the CV_ORDER_HEADER_TF calculation view*

The Auto Map By Name functionality creates input parameters with the same technical names as in a source object. Moreover, mapping between the source and the target is automatically managed. If needed, we can then adjust the properties of the created parameters. After defining the mapping and calculation view output structure, we can proceed with the activation. Afterward, it is worth testing the input parameters for the newly created view. The data preview should display a prompt with two input parameters (IP_LANGU and IP_CALENDAR). Results for the CM_DELV_DATE_DIFF_WD and STATUS_DESC columns should change according to the inserted values.

Update the Source Calculation View for the Order-Header CompositeProvider

As a next step, we need to update the BW/4HANA objects. If we want to keep the existing report in the current form, we could create a new composite provider and query, but in our scenario we want to update existing BW objects. This means that for the ZCPEXT02 CompositeProvider we need to replace the source CV_ORDER_HEADER calculation view with the newly created CV_ORDER_HEADER_TF view.

To adjust the source view for the ZCPEXT02 CompositeProvider, open the object and switch to the Scenario tab. Then hover over the existing calculation view and click the Replace button (Figure 3-43).

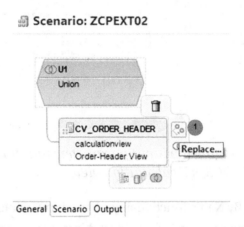

Figure 3-43. *Replacing the source view for the ZCPEXT02 CompositeProvider*

When clicking the Replace button, the system will open the window for searching the object for replacement. After selecting the new target view (CV_ORDER_HEADER_TF), the system will replace the previous view with the new one. For columns and input parameters that have the same technical names, mapping between the source and the target will remain unchanged. The rest of the mappings need to be managed manually. Figure 3-44 shows the updated target structure and the mapping for the ZCPEXT02 CompositeProvider.

The replacement of the view caused that CM_DELV_DATE field from the Target section to lose the assignment. This is because the measure derived from CV_ORDER_HEADER_TF has a different technical name (CM_DELV_DATE_DIFF_WD), so we need to create the missing assignment manually. The input parameter (IP_CALENDAR) should also be dragged to the Target section of the CompositeProvider structure because we want to use it as a reference for the new query variable. The final structure of the ZCPEXT02 CompositeProvider should look like Figure 3-44.

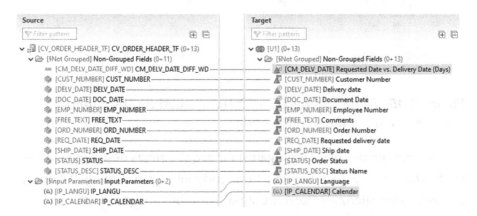

Figure 3-44. *Updating the structure of the ZCPEXT02 CompositeProvider*

Update the Query for the Order-Header Data with New Input Parameters

The last step to accomplish a task from Case Study 4 is to update the ZCPEXT02_Q01 query. For the newly mapped IP_CALENDAR parameter, we need to follow the same steps as we did for the IP_LANGU input parameter (the steps presented in Figures 3-27 to 3-32). The final filter definition for the ZCPEXT02_Q01 query should look like Figure 3-45.

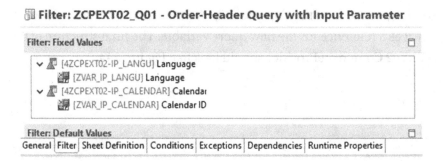

Figure 3-45. *Mapping the 4ZCPEXT02-IP_CALENDAR input parameter field to the query variable*

Now we can test the query against the requirements described in Case Study 4 by running the report in a front-end tool. When opening the query in Analysis for Microsoft Excel, we should now be prompted with two variables, as in Figure 3-46.

Order Number	Requested delivery date	Ship date	Order Status	Status Name	Requested Date vs. Delivery Date (Days)
0000000001	27.08.2004	19.08.2004	001	Delivered	-1
0000000007	06.09.2004	01.09.2004	001	Delivered	1
0000000015	17.09.2004	#	002	In Process	0

Prompts

Use Variant   Save the document on the server to enable use of variants

Prompt Summary   Specify Value for Prompts

Search variables...   **Order-Header Query with Input Parameter**

Order-Header Query with Input Parameter

* Language: E   * [ZVAR_IP_LANGU] Language   E

* Calendar ID: US   * [ZVAR_IP_CALENDAR] Calendar ID   US

Figure 3-46. *Updated Analysis for Microsoft Excel prompts for the ZCPEXT02_Q01 query*

The Status Name and Requested Date vs. Delivery Date (Days) columns will return output according to the values entered on the selection screen for the Language and Calendar ID variables. This means that the requirements from Case Study 4 have now been successfully fulfilled.

Summary

In this chapter, I described scenarios where the requirement was to expose data residing in HANA tables to the BW/4HANA layer. By taking advantage of field-based modeling and virtualization, we were able to create BW/4HANA reports without loading data into BW/4HANA modeling objects and also avoiding creating any single InfoObject.

In Case Study 1, I presented how easily we can provision data from a HANA table to a BW/4HANA query. In this scenario, we utilized two BW/4HANA modeling objects: Open ODS View and CompositeProvider.

Case Study 2 required us to combine two HANA tables before creating the final output. To achieve that, we brought into play an additional HANA modeling object called a calculation view. This helped us to join these two tables to create a dataset in the desired form before bringing it to the BW/4HANA layer.

In Case Study 3, I demonstrated how to pass values from query variables to calculation view input parameters. We learned that calculation views with input parameters should be consumed directly by CompositeProviders (the Open ODS View layer needs to be skipped in such a scenario).

The last scenario helped us to understand the usage of table functions. By going through the requirements from Case Study 4, we learned how to consume a calculation view in a table function. What is more, we walked through the examples of passing input parameter values between a calculation view and a table function in both directions. As a final result, you also learned how to pass query variable values into the table function SQL code.

Creating Field-Based BW/4HANA Models

Now that we have discussed the possibility of exposing HANA objects (tables and views) in Chapter 3, this chapter explains how to implement a BW/4HANA data model using a field-based approach. We already know that by utilizing Open ODS Views objects, we can bring external data located in the SAP HANA database schema to the BW/4HANA layer. In this chapter, we will take advantage of Open ODS Views to build a virtual star schema, field-based data model in BW. I will also explain how you can automatically generate an intermediate data storage layer between the Open ODS View and source objects, without needing to edit the reporting layer.

Scenario

After successful implementation of the basic data provisioning report for the orders data (Chapter 3), a project manager requested to build in BW/4HANA a proof of concept for a star schema data model. The requirement is to implement the data model in the BW/4HANA system, based on the tables replicated in the SAP HANA database schema. Two tables (ORDER_HEADER and ORDER_STATUS) were already used for

© Konrad Załęski 2021
K. Załęski, *Data Modeling with SAP BW/4HANA 2.0*,
https://doi.org/10.1007/978-1-4842-7089-9_4

building data provisioning reports in Chapter 3. The virtual model should include five external tables in total. Two of them are the fact tables.

- *Order Header*: This contains the order header information such as status, order date, customer number, and employee responsible.

- *Order Details*: This table is linked to the Order Header table and contains information on the order item level such as product ID or quantity ordered.

The remaining three tables are dimension/text tables.

- *Order Status*: This is a text table used to look up the status ID in the status description. It supports descriptions in two languages (English and German).

- *Products*: This is a dimension table containing information about product attributes.

- *Categories*: This is a text table that has information about the available group of products and its descriptions.

Figure 4-1 shows the logical data model for non-SAP tables replicated in the SAP HANA database.

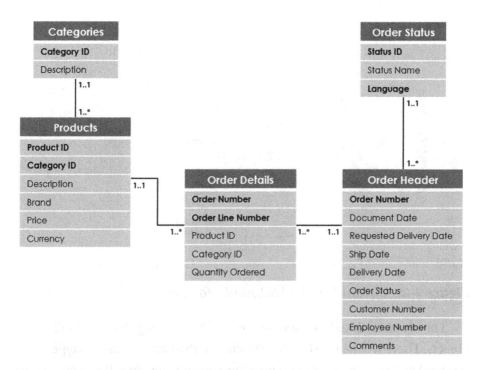

Figure 4-1. *Logical data model for Orders*

As shown in Figure 4-1, the data model consists of five tables. The connectors between the tables define their relationships. In the given example, all the relationships are of the one-to-many type (1..1 – 1..*). Each entity consists of a table header and a list of fields. Fields, which are in bold, indicate the primary key for a table. In the book's appendix you will find the SQL scripts to re-create all these tables in your local schema, in case you want to follow along with the demonstrated activities.

In the next sections of this chapter, I will show you how to implement the virtual data model in BW/4HANA using the given logical model as a reference (Figure 4-1). In this scenario, we will follow the Open ODS View-based modeling concept presented in Figure 2-7 (in Chapter 2). Figure 4-2 presents the general approach for implementing the Orders data model based on the requirements described in the scenario.

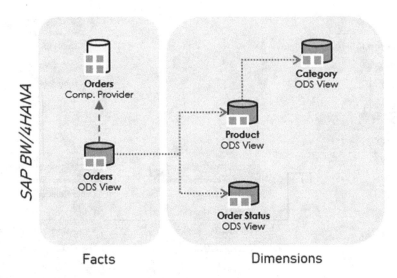

Figure 4-2. *Virtual BW/4HANA model for Orders*

The idea here is to build a virtual model by utilizing Open ODS View objects. There will be one Open ODS View of the Facts semantics type (Orders) and one Open ODS View of the Master Data type (Product). Since the Order Status and Category tables contain only keys and descriptions, the semantics type will be set to Texts. On top of the model, I will create a CompositeProvider, which will later be consumed by the query. First I will focus on implementing the Master Data/Texts objects.

Create the Dimension Calculation Views

We could start implementing Open ODS Views directly on the HANA tables, but as I mentioned previously, I prefer to consume tables with a calculation view first. This gives us more flexibility in case we need to apply any field conversion or additional calculation in the future. For each dimension/text table, I created a calculation view with a Dimension type (Figure 4-3).

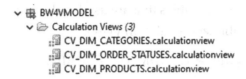

Figure 4-3. *List of dimension calculation views for a virtual data model*

As you will notice in Figure 4-3, I created a new HANA package called BW4VMODEL. This helps to keep the developments transparent and separated from other HANA objects, which were developed for different purposes. The calculation views listed under the BW4VMODEL package have the Dimension type. They do not contain any joins or calculations, but simply provision the data in the same structure as the underlying tables. As an example, you can see the structure of the CV_DIM_PRODUCTS calculation view in Figure 4-4.

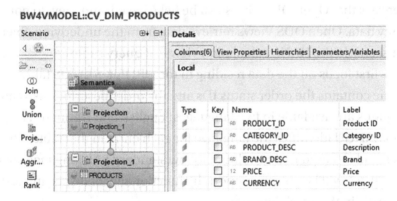

Figure 4-4. *CV_DIM_PRODUCTS calculation view definition*

Two remaining calculation views (for the Order Status and Category tables) follow the same approach. They consist of a Projection node pointing to the source table, from which all the fields are propagated to the

Semantics node. Here are tables that are used as the source for a specific calculation view (Table ➤ Calculation View):

- CATEGORIES ➤ CV_DIM_CATEGORIES

- ORDER_STATUS ➤ CV_DIM_ORDER_STATUSES

- PRODUCTS ➤ CV_DIM_PRODUCTS

Having these views validated and activated, we can now switch to the BW modeling perspective.

Create the Texts Open ODS Views

As visualized in Figure 4-2, for the given scenario there will be two Open ODS Views set to the Texts semantics type. Their purpose will be the same as the role of regular InfoObjects in classic EDW architecture. The main difference is that Open ODS Views can be field-based, and they do not store any data. Open ODS Views retrieve data from the underlying objects (in our scenario the HANA calculation views) at query runtime.

Let's first focus on the data residing in the ORDER_STATUS table. This table contains the order status IDs and the order descriptions. Status descriptions are available in two languages: English and German. The column LANGU identifies the language for each entry in that table. The values E and D stored in that column follow standard SAP language codes. As a result, we will be able to support the functionality of displaying text dynamically in the user's language.

The first Open ODS View will be sourcing data from the CV_DIM_ORDER_STATUSES calculation view. The Semantics type for this Open ODS View is set to Texts. In the Open ODS View editor, we need to specify the proper output structure. Figure 4-5 shows the output structure of the Order Status (ZTXT01) Open ODS View.

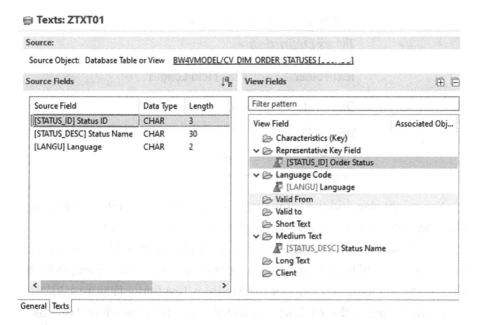

Figure 4-5. *Output structure of Order Status (ZTXT01) Open ODS View*

When defining the output structure of the Open ODS View, first we need to fill in the Representative Key field, which uniquely identifies each record. In our case, it is a STATUS_ID column. The second key of that table is the LANGU column; however, we have a dedicated folder for language codes.

Since the Order Status dimension will be language-dependent, we need to specify the column that will provision the language code values. In our case, we should put the LANGU column under the Language Code folder, as shown in Figure 4-5.

The last column that should be added to the output structure is the actual description field: STATUS_DESC. Depending on the source field length, it should be assigned under the proper Text-related folder. Table 4-1 specifies the maximum number of characters supported, depending on Text folder type.

Table 4-1. *Open ODS View Text*
Types Definition

Text Folder	Max Field Length
Short Text	20
Medium Text	40
Long Text	5000

You might also add the same description field to multiple Text folders. This way, when showing, for example, Short Text, it will display only the first 20 characters of the string. If the source field length will be longer, the rest of the text will be cut off. In our scenario, the Status Name length is 30 characters, so I assigned it under the Medium Text folder (Figure 4-5). To check the output of the ZTXT01 Open ODS View, let's open it in Analysis for Microsoft Excel. Figure 4-6 displays the output of the Order Status Open ODS View.

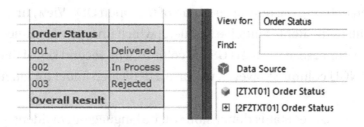

Figure 4-6. *Output of ZTXT01 in Analysis for Microsoft Excel*

You can notice that although the underlying ORDER_STATUS has six entries in total, the output of the ZTXT01 Open ODS View returns only three of them. This is because the default language for my BW user is set as EN, so entries that have the DE value in the LANGU column are skipped. If I changed the language to DE when logging into the BW/4HANA system, the descriptions would be returned in German.

Next, for the Categories dimension, we should follow the same steps as for the Order Status object. The only difference is that the CATEGORIES table is not language dependent, so we will not assign any column to the Language Code folder. Figure 4-7 shows the output structure of the ZTXT02 Category Open ODS View.

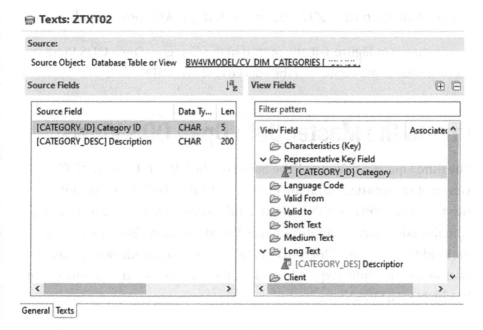

Figure 4-7. *Output structure of the Category (ZTXT02) Open ODS View*

The source CATEGORIES table consists only of a key and text fields. The CATEGORY_ID column has been put under the Representative Key Field section, while the CATEGORY_DESC field was dragged under the Long Text folder. Figure 4-8 presents the output of the Category Open ODS View.

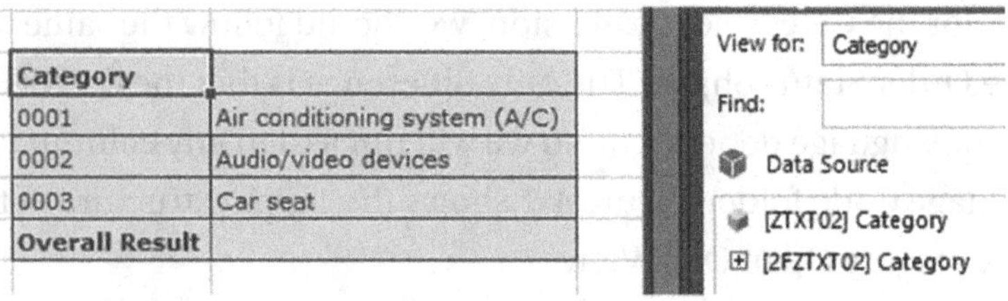

Figure 4-8. *Output of ZTXT02 in Analysis for Microsoft Excel*

As shown in Figure 4-8, the output of the Category Open ODS View corresponds to the content of the source CATEGORIES table.

Create the Master Data Open ODS Views

The third Open ODS View will be based on the CV_DIM_PRODUCTS view that sources data from the PRODUCTS table. Unlike the previous two tables, the PRODUCTS table, in addition to the key and text columns, contains additional attributes such as Brand and Price. Because of that, for Product during the Open ODS View creation we should select Master Data as the Semantics type. Figure 4-9 presents the output structure of the Product Open ODS View.

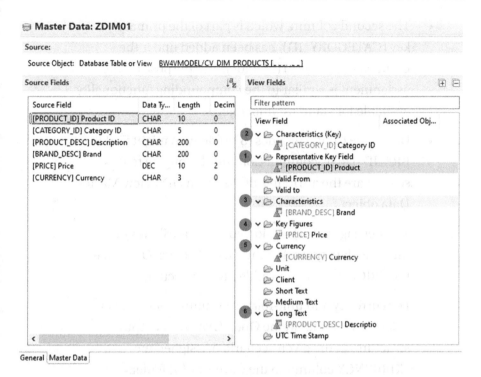

Figure 4-9. Initial output structure of the Product (ZDIM01) Open ODS View

In Figure 4-9, you can see how the source fields from the CV_DIM_ PRODUCTS calculation view (the Source Fields section) have been distributed between multiple folders (the View Fields section).

- The PRODUCTS table primary key consists of two columns: PRODUCT_ID and CATEGORY_ID. The Open ODS View supports a compounding functionality for objects that cannot be defined uniquely based on a single field. As shown in Figure 4-9, PRODUCT_ID is assigned to the Representative Key Field (1) folder.

- The second column, which is part of the primary key (CATEGORY_ID), has been added under the Characteristics (Key) (2) folder. The purpose of this assignment is similar to the compounding functionality available for standard InfoObjects.

- Under the Characteristics (3) folder you might find the BRAND_DESC column. Columns belonging to this section are the attributes of the Open ODS View Master Data object.

- The Key Figures (4) section contains attributes of numeric data types. For the ZDIM01 Open ODS View, the PRICE column was added to this section.

- For currency and unit-related columns there is also a dedicated folder in the Open ODS View output structure. In the given scenario, I assigned the CURRENCY column to the Currency (5) folder.

Note   When consuming currencies or units coming from an external data in Open ODS View, you need to be aware that BW/4HANA expects that all these values will be maintained in the central SAP currency and unit tables. Records with currency/unit values, which are not available in standard SAP tables, will not be supported.

- The Product Description column (PRODUCT_DESC) has been dragged to the Long Text (6) folder. This is because the PRODUCT_DESC column is 200 characters long.

Figure 4-10 presents an initial output of the Product Open ODS View.

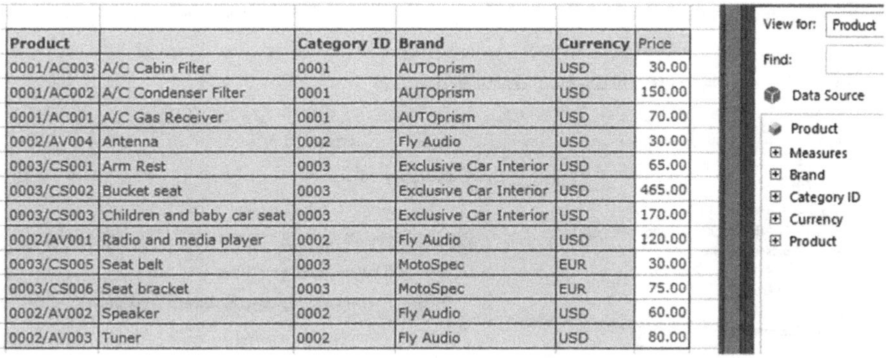

Product		Category ID	Brand	Currency	Price
0001/AC003	A/C Cabin Filter	0001	AUTOprism	USD	30.00
0001/AC002	A/C Condenser Filter	0001	AUTOprism	USD	150.00
0001/AC001	A/C Gas Receiver	0001	AUTOprism	USD	70.00
0002/AV004	Antenna	0002	Fly Audio	USD	30.00
0003/CS001	Arm Rest	0003	Exclusive Car Interior	USD	65.00
0003/CS002	Bucket seat	0003	Exclusive Car Interior	USD	465.00
0003/CS003	Children and baby car seat	0003	Exclusive Car Interior	USD	170.00
0002/AV001	Radio and media player	0002	Fly Audio	USD	120.00
0003/CS005	Seat belt	0003	MotoSpec	EUR	30.00
0003/CS006	Seat bracket	0003	MotoSpec	EUR	75.00
0002/AV002	Speaker	0002	Fly Audio	USD	60.00
0002/AV003	Tuner	0002	Fly Audio	USD	80.00

Figure 4-10. *Initial output of ZDIM01 in Analysis for Microsoft Excel*

The output of the Product Open ODS View contains all the columns derived from the source CV_DIM_PRODUCTS calculation view. Worth noting is that key values for the Product field consist of Product ID and Category ID (i.e., 0001/AC003). This is because we added a CATEGORY_ID column into the Characteristic (Key) section (see Figure 4-9).

There are two minor adjustments that we can implement to provide even more information for the Product dimension. First, the Category field displays ID values, so the user doesn't know what the actual category value is. Moreover, the Price field displays numbers without currency codes (the currency codes are displayed as a separate column). Let's now switch back to the BW modeling tools. As you remember, we created the ZTXT02 Text Open ODS View for the category data (Figure 4-7). This object contains a mapping between the category ID and the category name. Now we can utilize ZTXT02 Open ODS View by applying an association to that object in the Product Open ODS View output structure. Figure 4-10 illustrates how to define the association between the Category field and ZTXT02 Open ODS View.

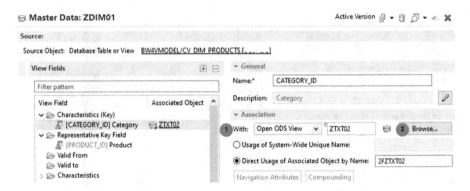

Figure 4-11. *Association for the Category field in the ZDIM01 Open ODS View*

To define the association between the field and the Open ODS View object, select the target field from the View Fields section. In the right pane, select the association type as Open ODS View. Then browse for the name of the Open ODS View, which you want to assign to that specific field. If you want to inherit the technical name of the associated object, select the Direct Usage of Associated Object by Name option. In the presented example (Figure 4-11), I assigned the ZTXT02 Open ODS View to the CATEGORY_ID field and selected the option to use the associated object by name. After defining the association, in the View Fields section you will find information about the associated object next to the field name (Open ODS View icon and its technical name).

The second adjustment that I wanted to apply was to assign the currency to the Price field. Click the PRICE field to display the Field Settings section (Figure 4-12).

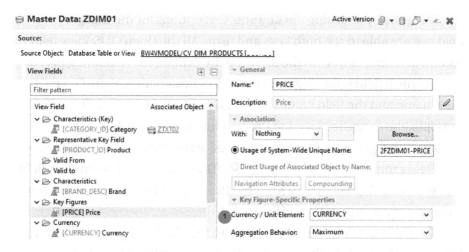

Figure 4-12. *Assigning the Currency element for the Price field in the ZDIM01 Open ODS View*

When you open the Currency / Unit Element drop-down, in the list you will see the fields that are available under the Currency folder. In my case, there will be only one column (CURRENCY). I will use that column as a currency element (Figure 4-12).

After applying these two changes, let's again execute the ZDIM01 object in Analysis for Microsoft Excel to validate the output. Figure 4-13 presents the output of the updated ZDIM01 object.

Product		Category		Price
0001/AC003	A/C Cabin Filter	0001	Air conditioning system (A/C)	$ 30.00
0001/AC002	A/C Condenser Filter	0001	Air conditioning system (A/C)	$ 150.00
0001/AC001	A/C Gas Receiver	0001	Air conditioning system (A/C)	$ 70.00
0002/AV004	Antenna	0002	Audio/video devices	$ 30.00
0003/CS001	Arm Rest	0003	Car seat	$ 65.00
0003/CS002	Bucket seat	0003	Car seat	$ 465.00
0003/CS003	Children and baby car seat	0003	Car seat	$ 170.00
0002/AV001	Radio and media player	0002	Audio/video devices	$ 120.00
0003/CS005	Seat belt	0003	Car seat	30.00 EUR
0003/CS006	Seat bracket	0003	Car seat	75.00 EUR
0002/AV002	Speaker	0002	Audio/video devices	$ 60.00
0002/AV003	Tuner	0002	Audio/video devices	$ 80.00

View for: Product

Find:

Data Source

- [ZDIM01] Product
- Measures
- [2FZDIM01-BRAND_DESC] Brand
- [2FZTXT02] Category
- [2FZDIM01-CURRENCY] Currency
- [2FZDIM01] Product

Figure 4-13. *Final output of ZDIM01 in Analysis for Microsoft Excel*

This time by choosing the Key and Text options for the Category field, we are able to see both keys and texts. All the Open ODS View field technical names start with the 2F string. By default, the remaining part of the technical field name is generated as a concatenation of the Open ODS View name and the field name (i.e., 2FZDIM01-BRAND_DESC). In our example, the exceptions are the Product and Category fields.

The name generated for fields that are assigned to the Representative Key Field group contain only the Open ODS View name. The Product field was set as the Representative Key field (see Figure 4-9); hence, its technical name is shown as 2FZDIM01 (Figure 4-13).

The Category field has associations to the ZTXT02 Open ODS View; hence, its name is inherited from that object. If we would like to keep the same naming convention as for other fields (2F<Open ODS View name>_<field name>), we should switch the selection from Direct Usage of Associated Object by Name to Usage of System-Wide Unique Name (Figure 4-11).

The second change that was implemented for the ZDIM01 Open ODS View refers to the Price field. The adjustment is also now reflected in the output shown in Figure 4-13. You can see that each value displayed in the Price column now has the currency code assigned.

Create the Transactional Calculation View

Like with dimension tables, I will create a virtual layer for the transactional data on the SAP HANA level first. In our data model, the transactional data is coming from two tables: ORDER_HEADER and ORDER_DETAILS. Both tables have an Order Number (ORD_NUMBER) column, and this column will be used to link header and item data into a single dataset. This table will be joined within the calculation view of the CUBE data category. Figure 4-14 presents the graphical editor of the CV_FACT_ORDERS View object.

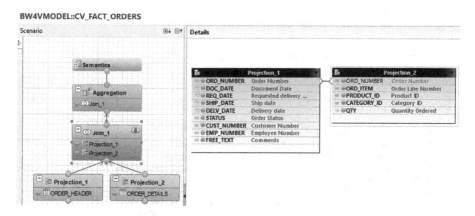

Figure 4-14. *CV_FACT_ORDERS calculation view definition*

The CV_FACT_ORDERS calculation view queries data from the Order
Header and Order Item tables (Projection_1 and Projection_2). Then
the Join node links these tables into a single dataset based on the ORD_
NUMBER column. From ORDER_HEADER, all columns are propagated
to the Semantics node. From ORDER_DETAILS, we also should select
all the fields except ORD_NUMBER, which is already derived from the
header table. When executing a data preview for the CV_FACT_ORDERS
calculation view, we should see the data from Header and Line Item
combined into a single dataset. This view will now be used as a source for
the Facts Open ODS View object.

Create the Facts Open ODS Views

After creating the Master Data and Texts BW/4HANA objects, now I
will create the central star schema object. As we already have Orders
transactional data combined into a single dataset, we can now define a new
Facts Open ODS View object. Remember that when defining a transactional
Open ODS View, you should select the Facts option as the Semantics type.
Figure 4-15 shows the initial setup of the ZFCT01 Open ODS View.

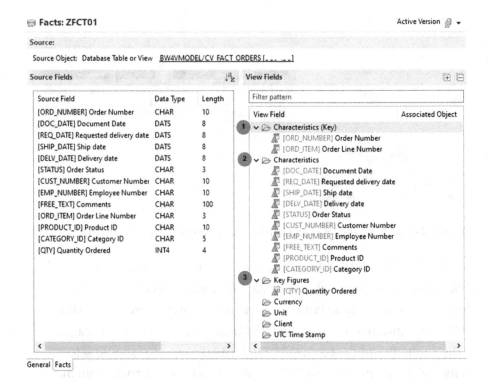

Figure 4-15. *Initial output structure of the Orders data (ZFCT01) Open ODS View*

The source fields available in the CV_FACT_ORDERS calculation view are distributed into these three categories:

- Order Number and Order Line Number are fields that form a composite key for the Orders data set. They uniquely define each Order Item record. Primary key fields are assigned to the Characteristics (Key) category (1).

Note   Primary key fields could be also assigned to the
Characteristics folder. However, if in the future there will be a need
to persist this data in an ADSO, by assigning primary key fields to
the Characteristics (Key) folder, we make sure that these fields will
automatically become key fields of the generated ADSO.

- Transactional data fields are grouped under the
  Characteristics folder (2). Most of the fields coming
  from the CV_FACT_ORDERS calculation view were
  added to this group.

- The Quantity Ordered (QTY) column is a cumulative
  measure; hence, it has been added to the Key Figures
  folder (3).

Let's now activate the ZFCT01 object to check what the content looks like.

Order Number	Order Line Number	Order Status	Category ID	Product ID	Quantity Ordered
0000000001	001	001	0001	AC001	25
0000000001	002	001	0001	AC002	30
0000000002	001	001	0002	AV004	13
0000000002	002	001	0003	CS002	2
0000000002	003	001	0003	CS006	19
0000000003	001	001	0002	AV003	25
0000000004	001	001	0002	AV004	30
0000000005	001	001	0002	AV004	6
0000000006	001	001	0003	CS005	14
0000000006	002	001	0001	AC003	18
0000000006	003	001	0002	AV001	21
0000000006	004	001	0002	AV004	35
0000000006	005	001	0003	CS002	7

Data Source

- [ZFCT01] Orders data
- Measures
- [2FZFCT01-CATEGORY_ID] Category ID
- [2FZFCT01-FREE_TEXT] Comments
- [2FZFCT01-CUST_NUMBER] Customer Number
- [2FZFCT01-DELV_DATE] Delivery date
- [2FZFCT01-DOC_DATE] Document Date
- [2FZFCT01-EMP_NUMBER] Employee Number
- [2FZFCT01-ORD_ITEM] Order Line Number
- [2FZFCT01-ORD_NUMBER] Order Number
- [2FZFCT01-STATUS] Order Status
- [2FZFCT01-PRODUCT_ID] Product ID
- [2FZFCT01-REQ_DATE] Requested delivery date
- [2FZFCT01-SHIP_DATE] Ship date

Figure 4-16. *Initial output of ZFCT01 in Analysis for Microsoft Excel*

In Figure 4-16 you might see the output of the ZFCT01 Open ODS View
for some selected fields. Currently, the Order Status, Category, and Product
fields display values as keys, which might not be meaningful for the end
users unless they know what the specific ID stands for. As we now have

the initial setup of the Orders transactional Open ODS View ready, we can enhance the fields by applying associations. Thanks to that, some of the fields will inherit properties of the associated Texts/Master Data Open ODS Views that were created in previous sections of this chapter.

The CV_FACT_ORDERS calculation view displays the Order Status and Category values as keys. To also enable descriptions for the reporting, we can utilize the Order Status (ZTXT01) and Category (ZTXT02) Open ODS Views and apply associations to the STATUS and CATEGORY fields accordingly. Follow the same steps that were presented in Figure 4-11 for the Category field to define an association in the ZFCT01 Open ODS View. Figure 4-17 shows associations between transactional fields and Texts Open ODS Views objects.

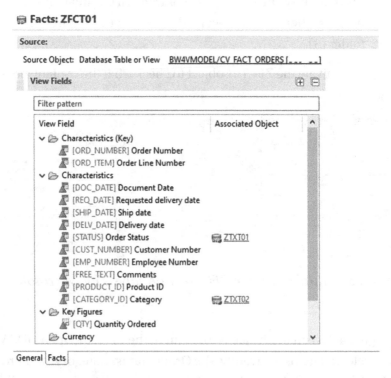

Figure 4-17. Association for the Category and Order Status fields in the ZFCT01 Open ODS View

The Category and Order Status fields shown in Figure 4-17 now have associations to text Open ODS Views. In the previous section, we created a Master Data object for the Product dimension. As you remember, this dimension has a compounded key, which consists of the Product ID and Category ID fields. When assigning the Product (ZDIM01) Open ODS View, we need to keep that in mind.

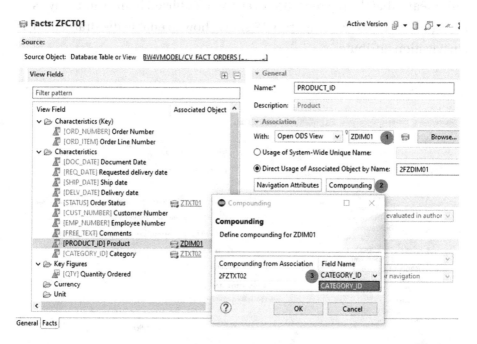

Figure 4-18. *Association for the Product field in the ZFCT01 Open ODS View*

After applying an association between the PRODUCT_ID field and the ZDIM01 Open ODS View, we also need to define compounding for this Open ODS View. By clicking the Compounding button (Figure 4-18), we will be able to select the second field used for association. In the given scenario, we should select the CATEGORY_ID field as a compound field. There might be a case when your master data Open ODS View compounded key consists of more than two fields. In such a case when making associations, you need to make sure that compounding is defined for each master data Open ODS View key field. Once we have assigned the master data Open ODS View to our Product field, we can select master data navigation attributes. In the Product Open ODS View, we defined the Brand field as a characteristic (Figure 4-9). All fields that are defined as Open ODS View characteristics can be later used as navigation attributes. This means that during reporting they can be utilized in the same way as all regular output fields. Figure 4-19 shows how to enable the Brand field as a navigation attribute.

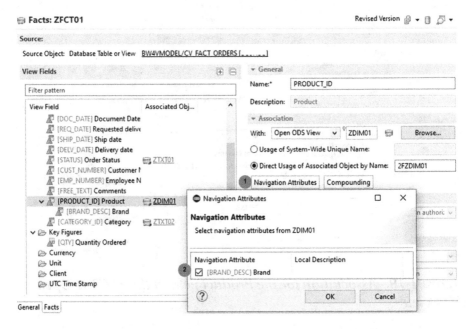

Figure 4-19. *Selecting the navigation attribute for ZFCT01 Open ODS View*

When clicking the Navigation Attributes button, we will see the list of characteristics available for the associated Master Data object. By selecting the check box next to the given attribute, we can add them as a navigation attribute. In our scenario, the Product Open ODS View (ZDIM01) has only one characteristic defined. After selecting the BRAND_DESC field, you will notice it is added to the View Fields section under the PRODUCT_ID field.

Since all the adjustments are now in place, let's now validate the output of the ZFCT01 Open ODS View for selected fields (Figure 4-20).

Order Number	Order Line Number	Order Status	Category	Product	Quantity Ordered
0000000001	001	Delivered	Air conditioning system (A/C)	A/C Gas Receiver	25
0000000001	002	Delivered	Air conditioning system (A/C)	A/C Condenser Filter	30
0000000002	001	Delivered	Audio/video devices	Antenna	13
0000000002	002	Delivered	Car seat	Bucket seat	2
0000000002	003	Delivered	Car seat	Seat bracket	19

Figure 4-20. Final output of ZFCT01 in Analysis for Microsoft Excel

This time when opening the Orders Open ODS View in Analysis for Microsoft Excel (Figure 4-20), in the fields for which we defined associations, text is set as a default display. Another advantage is that we can now utilize the attributes of the Product dimension (see Figure 4-21).

Product	Brand	Currency	Price	Quantity Ordered
A/C Cabin Filter	AUTOprism	USD	USD 30,00	26
A/C Condenser Filter	AUTOprism	USD	USD 150,00	47
A/C Gas Receiver	AUTOprism	USD	USD 70,00	53
Antenna	Fly Audio	USD	USD 30,00	84
Bucket seat	Exclusive Car Interior	USD	USD 465,00	9
Children and baby car seat	Exclusive Car Interior	USD	USD 170,00	40
Radio and media player	Fly Audio	USD	USD 120,00	70
Seat belt	MotoSpec	EUR	30,00 EUR	66
Seat bracket	MotoSpec	EUR	75,00 EUR	42
Tuner	Fly Audio	USD	USD 80,00	25

Data Source
- [ZFCT01] Orders data [DS_1]
- Measures
- [2FZDIM01=BRAND_DESC] Brand
- [2FZTXT02] Category
- [2FZFCT01-FREE_TEXT] Comments
- [2FZFCT01-CUST_NUMBER] Customer Number
- [2FZFCT01-DELV_DATE] Delivery date
- [2FZFCT01-DOC_DATE] Document Date
- [2FZFCT01-EMP_NUMBER] Employee Number
- [2FZFCT01-ORD_ITEM] Order Line Number
- [2FZFCT01-ORD_NUMBER] Order Number
- [2FZTXT01] Order Status
- [2FZDIM01] Product
  - Members
  - Attributes
    - [2FZDIM01-BRAND_DESC] Brand
    - [2FZDIM01-CURRENCY] Currency
    - [2FZDIM01-PRICE] Price

Figure 4-21. Display of Product attributes for ZFCT01 in Analysis for Microsoft Excel

First, you might notice that there is a new Brand field available for navigation. This field was not available in the initial output of ZFCT01 (Figure 4-16). This is because we set this field as a navigation attribute (Figure 4-19). Other product-related information such as Currency and Price are visible under the Attributes section of the Product (2FZDIM01) field. Unlike the navigation attribute (2FZDIM01=BRAND_DESC), display attributes cannot be used for individual drill-down, but only together with the main characteristic (in this case with Product). Although the Brand field was set as a navigation attribute, it will also be visible as a Product attribute. On the left side of Figure 4-21, you can see the output of the Product display attributes.

Create the CompositeProvider Consuming the Open ODS View

Before creating a query, I will create a CompositeProvider, which consumes the Orders data (ZFCT01) Open ODS View. Thanks to that, in the future I will be able to include additional objects by using the CompositeProvider Join and/or Union nodes. Figure 4-22 shows how the ZCPFCT01 CompositeProvider was modeled.

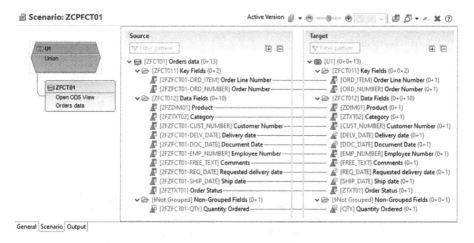

Figure 4-22. *Defining the structure of the ZCPFCT01*
CompositeProvider

In the CompositeProvider named ZCPFCT01, all the source fields have
been mapped to the output. Although the Brand field was enabled in the
underlying Open ODS View (ZFCT01) as a navigation attribute, it is not
visible here by default. If we want to enable the navigation attribute, we
should go to the Output tab. This tab shows a list of the CompositeProvider
output fields. Here we can enable the navigation attributes if available.

As shown in Figure 4-23, associations to the Master Data/Texts Open
ODS Views are inherited from the consumed ZFCT01 object. By right-
clicking the Product characteristic, we have an option to define navigation
attributes to be included in the output. In the opened window, we will see
the list of available fields that can be added as navigation attributes. In our
scenario, there will be only one attribute available for the selection. After
selecting the Brand field as a navigation attribute, it will be visible under
the main Product characteristic (as in Figure 4-23). As this setup is the
desired one, we can now activate the CompositeProvider.

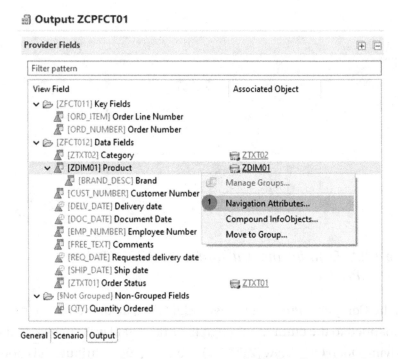

Figure 4-23. *Adding the navigation attribute for the ZCPFCT01 CompositeProvider*

Note   If you see a "column view" error during the CompositeProvider activation, run the RSDDB_LOGINDEX_CREATE program again for the underlying Open ODS View to create a column view (see Figure 3-12).

After the successful activation of the CompositeProvider, you can create a final query on top. When defining a query structure (Figure 4-24), you will be able to use all the fields from the ZCPFCT01 CompositeProvider including navigation attributes.

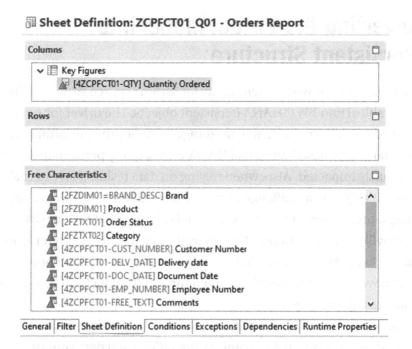

Figure 4-24. *Definition of the ZCPFCT01_Q01 query*

In this scenario, we have built a virtual data model based on Open ODS Views. Since the underlying tables are stored in the HANA database, we did not have to persist this data on the BW/4HANA layer. However, there are scenarios where the underlying data model is much more complex and requires many additional operations and calculations. Also, data does not always reside in HANA tables but can be queried from external databases through Smart Data Access. In such cases, we might need to create an additional staging layer to avoid performance issues at query runtime. In the next section, I will describe how to generate an intermediate BW/4HANA persistent layer for the existing Open ODS View objects.

Converting the Virtual Model into a Persistent Structure

Open ODS Views provide functionality for turning source structures (like remote tables) into BW/4HANA persistent objects. The driver for switching the virtual model to persistent data storage is usually the performance. If the model is fully based on virtual HANA tables, query performance will be obviously impacted. Also, when relying on data residing on external systems, it might be a challenge to ensure the stability of the virtual model. During source system downtimes, external data exposed through BW models will not be accessible at all. To avoid that, you might prefer to load source data to BW objects so that in the case of any connection or external system downtimes, the model will still return all the data from before the last successful load request.

Also, when you want to combine external tables with various BW objects, due to the number of complex operations and data volume, running the query on the fly may take some time. Scenarios that need to support time-based data snapshots also cannot be maintained by using the virtual approach.

For these kinds of scenarios, the Open ODS Framework enables the functionality of switching from the virtual model to the persistent structures. This approach helps with performance-related issues. The conversion can be done independently for each Open ODS View, so you can decide for which Open ODS View you would like to persist the data. It is worth mentioning that even if you already have built the virtual model, you can generate the persistent layer without rebuilding the Open ODS Views and other objects that were already created on top of them (such as CompositeProviders and/or queries). Thanks to that, you can implement your data model using an iterative approach, starting from the fully virtual structures, making the first round of unit tests, and afterward choosing virtual objects for which it is required to generate data storage to improve the performance or to capture data snapshots.

As was mentioned in the first chapter, Open ODS Views are virtual modeling objects, so they do not store any data. However, they enable us to generate an ADSO-based data structure, including all the necessary BW/4HANA objects to transfer the data, such as the Data Source, Transformation, and DTP objects. To demonstrate the conversion from virtual structure to persistent object, I will use the ZFCT01 Open ODS View as a reference. Figure 4-25 depicts an overview of switching from virtual to persistent data structures for the Orders Open ODS View.

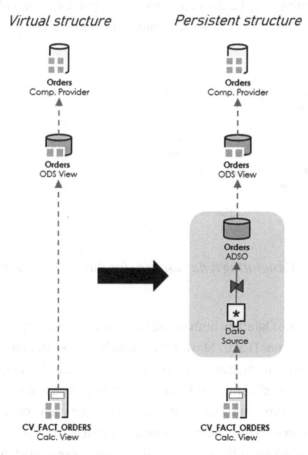

Figure 4-25. *Conversion of the Orders Open ODS View from a virtual to persistent structure*

As shown in Figure 4-25, in the virtual approach, the Orders data is queried directly from the underlying calculation view. Our goal is to convert the current data flow to utilize persistent structures.

The Open ODS View provides Generate Dataflow functionality, which makes this conversion easy to implement. As depicted in Figure 4-25, on the BW/4HANA side we will generate a few additional objects. These objects are Data Source, Transformation and DTP, and finally the Advanced DSO where the actual data will be stored.

To start converting the data flow, open the Open ODS View object and in the editor's General tab click the Generate Dataflow button (Figure 4-26).

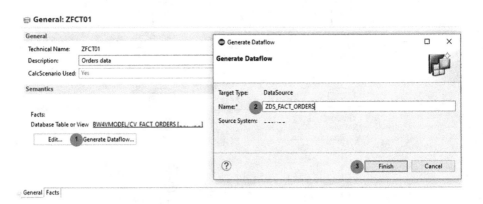

Figure 4-26. *Generating a data source for the ZFCT01 Open ODS View*

The Generate Dataflow button will be available for all Open ODS View semantic types (Facts, Master Data, and Texts), so depending on your needs, you can generate a persistent layer also for other Open ODS View objects. After clicking this button, Eclipse opens a window for providing the name of the Data Source object. Once you proceed, the new data source with the given name will be automatically created. You will notice that in the Semantics section of the given Orders data Open ODS View, the new ZDS_FACT_ORDERS BW data source replaces the former

CV_FACT_ORDERS calculation view (Figure 4-26). The created data source will extract data from the CV_FACT_ORDERS view, and its structure corresponds to the structure of that calculation view. The data types of the calculation view fields are converted into SAP BW/4HANA data types (see Figure 4-27).

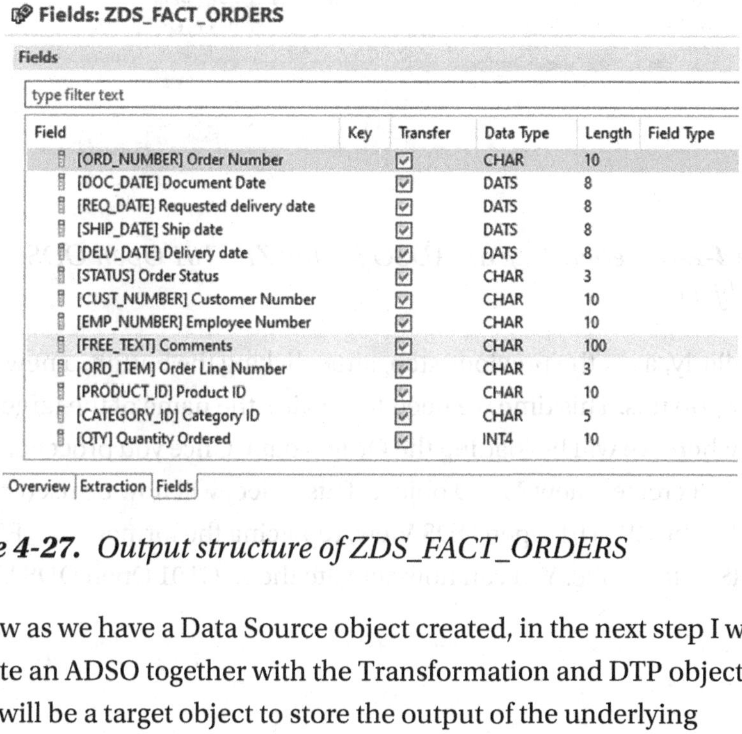

Fields: ZDS_FACT_ORDERS

Fields

type filter text

Field	Key	Transfer	Data Type	Length	Field Type
[ORD_NUMBER] Order Number		☑	CHAR	10	
[DOC_DATE] Document Date		☑	DATS	8	
[REQ_DATE] Requested delivery date		☑	DATS	8	
[SHIP_DATE] Ship date		☑	DATS	8	
[DELV_DATE] Delivery date		☑	DATS	8	
[STATUS] Order Status		☑	CHAR	3	
[CUST_NUMBER] Customer Number		☑	CHAR	10	
[EMP_NUMBER] Employee Number		☑	CHAR	10	
[FREE_TEXT] Comments		☑	CHAR	100	
[ORD_ITEM] Order Line Number		☑	CHAR	3	
[PRODUCT_ID] Product ID		☑	CHAR	10	
[CATEGORY_ID] Category ID		☑	CHAR	5	
[QTY] Quantity Ordered		☑	INT4	10	

Overview | Extraction | Fields

Figure 4-27. *Output structure of ZDS_FACT_ORDERS*

Now as we have a Data Source object created, in the next step I will generate an ADSO together with the Transformation and DTP objects. ADSO will be a target object to store the output of the underlying calculation view. Click the Generate Dataflow button again to create an ADSO (Figure 4-28).

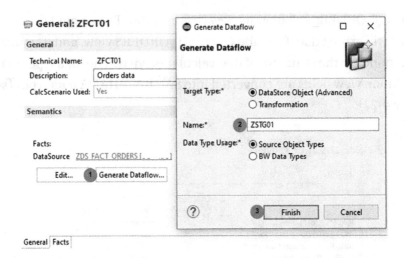

Figure 4-28. *Generating an ADSO for the ZFCT01 Open ODS View object*

Similarly, as in the previous step, after clicking the button, a new window pop ups. This time we need to provide the name of the target ADSO, where we will be loading the Orders data. Once you proceed, the system will create a new ADSO object. This object will now be used as a source for the ZFCT01 Open ODS View, replacing the former ZDS_FACT_ORDERS data source. You can now activate the ZFCT01 Open ODS View.

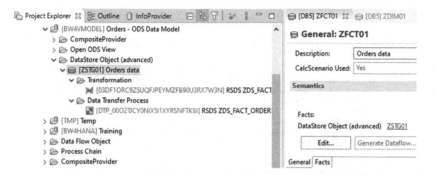

Figure 4-29. *Overview of generated objects for Orders data persistent structure*

As shown in Figure 4-29, in the Project Explorer you can see that in addition to the ZSTG01 ADSO object, the system automatically generated the transformation and DTP as well. By default the system creates the ADSO with the Staging DataStore Object type and the Compress Data option selected (for detailed information about ADSO types, check Chapter 1). If needed, you can manually adjust the ADSO settings according to your requirements. The output structure of the generated ADSO corresponds to the structure of the underlying ZDS_FACT_ORDERS data source (Figure 4-30).

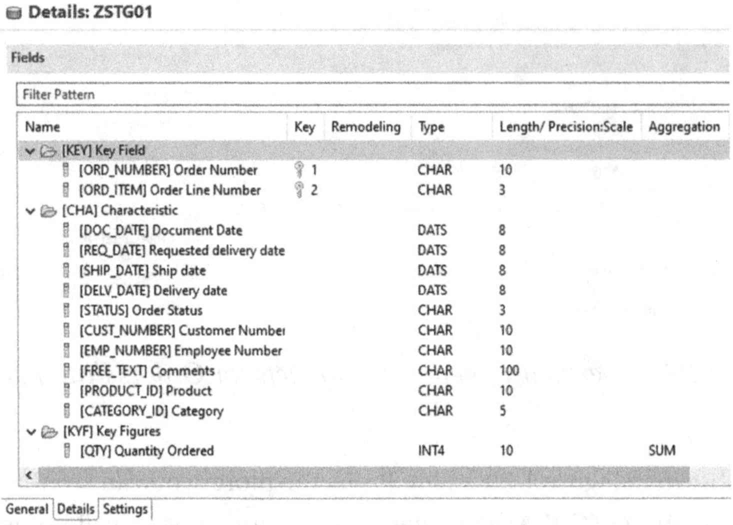

Details: ZSTG01

Fields

Filter Pattern

Name	Key	Remodeling	Type	Length/ Precision:Scale	Aggregation
∨ ▷ [KEY] Key Field					
[ORD_NUMBER] Order Number	1		CHAR	10	
[ORD_ITEM] Order Line Number	2		CHAR	3	
∨ ▷ [CHA] Characteristic					
[DOC_DATE] Document Date			DATS	8	
[REQ_DATE] Requested delivery date			DATS	8	
[SHIP_DATE] Ship date			DATS	8	
[DELV_DATE] Delivery date			DATS	8	
[STATUS] Order Status			CHAR	3	
[CUST_NUMBER] Customer Number			CHAR	10	
[EMP_NUMBER] Employee Number			CHAR	10	
[FREE_TEXT] Comments			CHAR	100	
[PRODUCT_ID] Product			CHAR	10	
[CATEGORY_ID] Category			CHAR	5	
∨ ▷ [KYF] Key Figures					
[QTY] Quantity Ordered			INT4	10	SUM

General | Details | Settings

Figure 4-30.   Output structure of the ZSTG01 ADSO

When generating the ADSO, the system will automatically identify key fields, based on the ZFCT01 Open ODS View fields, that were assigned to the Characteristics (Key) folder (Figure 4-15).

After completing the generation of all the necessary BW/4HANA objects, when trying to execute the existing ZCPFCT01_Q01 query, initially no applicable data will be found. To make the data available, you need to first load the output of the calculation view into the ADSO by executing the data transfer process shown in Figure 4-29. When you load the data to the ADSO, you don't need to apply any other changes on the CompositeProvider and Query levels.

Summary

In this chapter, I walked through a scenario where the goal was to create a BW/4HANA Orders data model that corresponds to a source relational data model. At first I implemented the virtual calculation view layer on the

HANA side. Although it is possible to build such a model directly on tables, the calculation view layer gives more flexibility if we need additional data manipulation on the source data.

By consuming these views, I was able to implement a fully virtual data model in the BW/4HANA system. The purpose of the underlying source object determined the type of Open ODS View that I used. To create a model, I took advantage of all three available types of Open ODS Views. These types are Texts, Master Data, and Facts. The virtual model was later consumed by the CompositeProvider and the final Query object.

At the end, I demonstrated how a virtual model can be easily converted into a persistent structure, without impacting any objects created on top of that model. The examples helped you understand what the limitations of the fully virtual models are and what scenarios enforce us to consider converting virtual models into persistent structures.

CHAPTER 5

Creating a Hybrid Data Model

In the previous chapter, we created a field-based data model, which was constructed based on Open ODS View objects. As a next step, I will guide you through a scenario where we will be mixing the field-based approach with regular InfoObjects to implement a hybrid data model. I will highlight the benefits as well as the limitations and disadvantages of the hybrid modeling approach.

Scenario

The next requirement for the Orders data model is to enhance it with additional attributes. This time, the business user asked to have the ability to utilize the master data of existing SAP InfoObjects. There are two InfoObjects that should be incorporated into the existing data model:

- *0CALDAY (Calendar Day)*: This is a standard SAP InfoObject containing time-related attributes and hierarchies. The user wants to be able to take advantage of the 0CALDAY master data for the Document Date column, which currently displays only date values.

© Konrad Załęski 2021
K. Załęski, *Data Modeling with SAP BW/4HANA 2.0*,
https://doi.org/10.1007/978-1-4842-7089-9_5

- *ZBW4CUST (Customer)*: This is a custom SAP
  InfoObject containing customer information. The
  master data of ZBW4CUST will not cover all the
  customer numbers that are available in the external data
  model. Business users want to have the ability to utilize
  customer attributes for customer numbers that are
  common. For those customers, which are not available
  in the ZBW4CUST object, the attributes will not be
  maintained and should be kept blank. The Customer
  InfoObject contains these three navigation attributes:

  - ZBW4ADDR (address)

  - ZBW4STAT (state)

  - ZBW4COMP (company name)

  Figure 5-1 presents the content and attributes of the
  Customer InfoObject.

Data Grid			Key Figures	Number of Records
Customer	Company Name	Address	State	
100000010	Mobile Garage	190 College Avenue	New York	1
100000011	EmpireCab	3384 Edgewood Avenue	Georgia	1
100000013	Blue Moto	3028 Tanglewood Road	Ohio	1
#	#	#	#	1
Result	Result	Result	Result	4

Figure 5-1. *Content of the Customer InfoObject*

As shown in Figure 5-1, the master data of the
Customer InfoObjects contains only three customer
numbers. Customers 0100000014 and 0100000015,
which are available in the external ORDER_
HEADER table, are not part of this InfoObject.

To achieve the requested functionality, I will follow the hybrid modeling approach. Figure 5-2 depicts how the existing model will be extended to fulfill the business requirements.

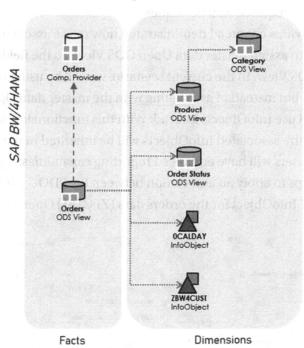

Figure 5-2. *Hybrid data model for the Orders data*

As shown in Figure 5-2, to fulfill the business needs, we will enhance the existing Orders data model by applying additional associations to InfoObjects. This way, we will be able to take advantage of that master data that is available in SAP InfoObjects.

Defining Associations with the OCALDAY InfoObject

The first business requirement is to include a time dimension in the existing data model for the Document Date column. Users requested the ability for additional time attributes for this column, such as calendar year,

191

quarter, month, and week. In addition, users wanted to take advantage of time hierarchies. To achieve that, we can incorporate an 0CALDAY standard InfoObject into the Orders data model. This InfoObject already contains all the required functionalities.

In the previous chapter, I demonstrated how to use association functionality to assign master data Open ODS Views to the fields of the Fact Open ODS View. In the current scenario, we will be using the same functionality, but instead of associating with the master data Open ODS Views, we will use InfoObjects instead. With this functionality, all the properties of the associated InfoObjects will be inherited in the output field; hence, users will have enhanced reporting capabilities. Figure 5-3 shows the steps to apply an association between the 0DOC_DATE field and the 0CALDAY InfoObject for the orders data (ZFCT01) Open ODS View.

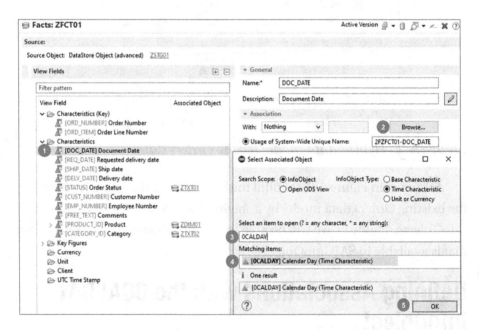

Figure 5-3. *Association for the Document Date field in the ZFCT01 Open ODS View object*

To apply an association between the output field and the InfoObject, select the target field from the View Fields section. From the right pane, click the Browse (2) button. This will open a window where you can search (3) for the target InfoObject, which you want to use for the association. When you find the target InfoObject, select it (4) and click OK (5). Once you have applied the associations, you can specify the navigation attributes that you want to enable from the associated InfoObject for the reporting.

As shown in Figure 5-4, for the DOC_DATE column I selected three navigation attributes that are coming from the associated 0CALDAY InfoObject. These attributes are 0CALMONTH, 0CALYEAR, and 0CALWEEK. In the Local Description column, you can provide your description for navigation attributes. It can help you to easily identify the referenced field.

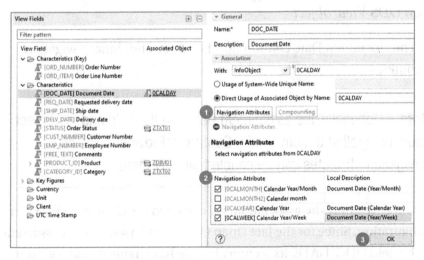

Figure 5-4. *Adding 0CALDAY navigation attributes for the ZFCT01 Open ODS View object*

Figure 5-5 presents the target configuration for the Document Date column.

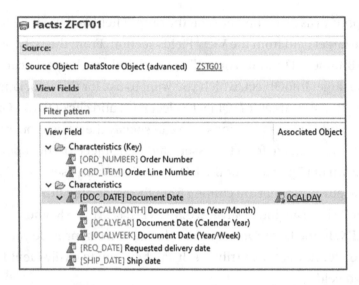

Figure 5-5.   0CALDAY navigation attributes in the ZFCT01 Open ODS View object

The Document Date column now has three additional navigation attributes.

Note   Optionally, the assignment between the field and InfoObject could be applied directly on the CompositeProvider level. Also, navigation attributes can be enabled directly there.

Once we apply the association, we can go to the CompositeProvider configuration. Since for the fact Open ODS View I used a direct association for the field DOC_DATE, its technical name has changed, and we need adjust the mapping in the ZCPFCT01 CompositeProvider (unless we created a new CompositeProvider). In addition, we want to add new navigation attributes to the output structure of the CompositeProvider for the Orders data.

As you can see in Figure 5-6, the Document Date column (highlighted) in the Target section shows a warning. Because of the change to the technical name of that column, the assignment from Source to Target has been removed. This column should now be removed from the Target section and replaced with the 0CALDAY column. What is worth noting is that by default you cannot see the navigation attributes that were enabled for the Document Date column at the Open ODS View level. To display them, in the Source section, right-click the Open ODS View name and select Show Unassigned Navigation Attributes (Figure 5-6).

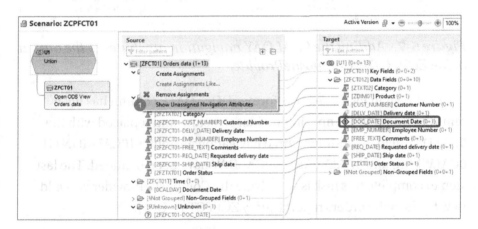

Figure 5-6. *Show Unassigned Navigation Attributes menu item in CompositeProvider*

After displaying the navigation attributes, you are able to map them from Source to Target (Figure 5-7).

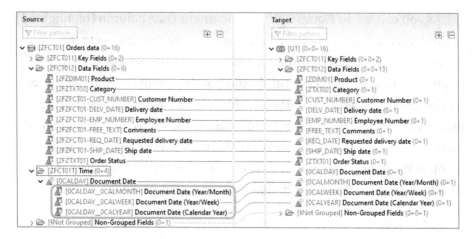

Figure 5-7. *Adding the 0CALDAY navigation attributes to the output of the ZCPFCT01 CompositeProvider*

As shown in Figure 5-7, the former DOC_DATE column has been removed from the CompositeProvider structure and replaced with the 0CALDAY field. In addition, three navigation attributes (0CALMONTH, 0CALWEEK, and 0CALYEAR) of 0CALDAY have been included. The last step to complete this task is to activate the CompositeProvider and add new fields to the orders report (query ZCPFCT01_Q01).

Note   If you see a "column view" error during the CompositeProvider activation, run the RSDDB_LOGINDEX_CREATE program for the underlying Open ODS View to create a column view (see Figure 3-12).

Figure 5-8 shows the new fields that have been added to the query ZCPFCT01_Q01.

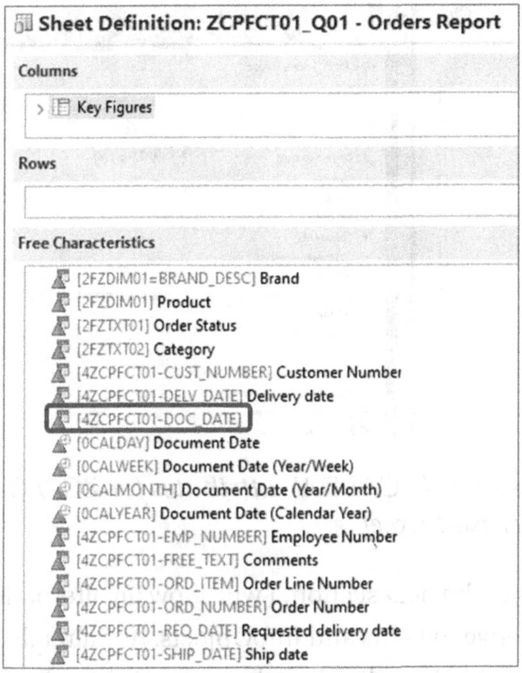

Figure 5-8. Adding the 0CALDAY navigation attributes to the output of the ZCPFCT01_Q01 query

Like we did for the ZCPFCT01 CompositeProvider, we first need to remove the obsolete DOC_DATE column, which has been replaced with the 0CALDAY InfoObject (Figure 5-8). Then we can add the 0CALWEEK, 0CALMONTH, and 0CALYEAR columns and save the query. Now when running the report in Analysis for Microsoft Excel, we can take advantage of the new time attributes as well as the hierarchies.

You can see (Figure 5-9) that in the orders report users can now navigate using the Calendar Year, Year/Month, and Year/Week columns. In addition, they can take advantage of the hierarchies that are available under the 0CALDAY InfoObject. As an example, I used the Year-Quarter-Month-Date hierarchy to see the totals for Quantity Ordered, broken down by Year, Quarter, Month, and Date. This gives users new display, grouping, and filtering capabilities when working with reports and dashboards.

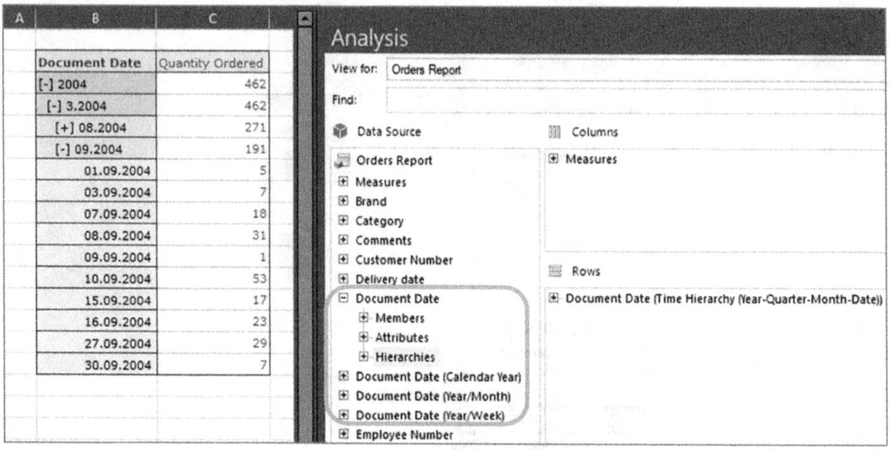

Figure 5-9. *Display of 0CALDAY attributes for ZCPFCT01_Q01 in Analysis for Microsoft Excel*

Before going to the next section, I will show an alternative way to define an association between fields and InfoObjects. As I already mentioned, the association can be applied also directly on the CompositeProvider level. In the next example, I assigned the 0CALDAY InfoObject to the Delivery Date (DELV_DATE) column, which is another field of a date type. The steps for assigning InfoObjects to the field at a CompositeProvider level are the same as demonstrated for Open ODS Views (Figure 5-3). Once the association is added, you can enable navigation attributes by right-clicking the field and selecting the Navigation Attributes option.

Figure 5-10 shows that the field DELV_DATE now also has an association with the 0CALDAY InfoObject. In addition, you can see that there is an option to enable navigation attributes. After selecting navigation attributes, they are shown under the DELV_DATE column.

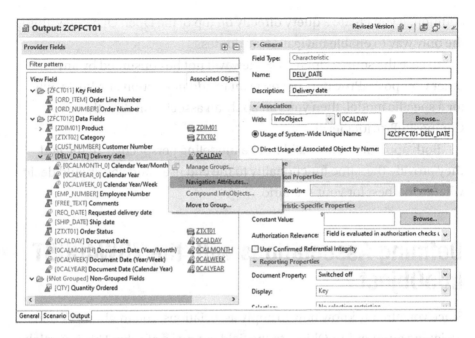

Figure 5-10. Adding 0CALDAY navigation attributes for ZCPFCT01 CompositeProvider

Note When using association functionality, you need to remember that for a single InfoObject, the option Direct Usage of Associated Object by Name can be set for only one field within the CompositeProvider. If you need to apply an association for a specific InfoObject for multiple columns, you should keep the option Usage of System-Wide Unique Name.

If the source fact Open ODS View will be reused in multiple models, then as a good practice it is recommended to apply an association in that object already. Thanks to that, every time when it is consumed by the CompositeProvider, all relevant fields are already available. Otherwise, you would need to configure associations for every new CompositeProvider. In addition, if you create a query directly on top of the Open ODS View, this is the only way to enable navigation attributes.

In case the source Open ODS View will not be consumed by any other CompositeProviders or you want to add navigation attributes only for a specific model, then you can apply an association directly on a CompositeProvider level.

Both approaches are valid from a modeling perspective. In the end, they provide the same functionality to the end user, and you should decide what works best for your scenario.

Defining Associations with the ZBW4CUST InfoObject

Since you already know how to apply associations, you might think that assigning another InfoObject to the field is a piece of cake. This is partially true; however, for the second requirement, we need to consider additional constraints.

When applying an association between the Document Date field and the 0CALDAY InfoObject, we do not need to worry about the data consistency between these objects. This is because the DATE data type for the Document Date column already constrains the values that this column might take (only dates). Thanks to that, we avoid the situation when the Document Date column contains a value that is not available in the 0CALDAY InfoObject. For the Customer field, the situation is different. Customer data is maintained in the external data source; hence, we cannot ensure that IDs will always match the ZBW4CUST InfoObject master data. As described in the scenario, the ORDER_HEADER table contains two customer numbers that are not part of the ZBW4CUST InfoObject master data. See the comparison of the Customer master data values to the distinct values of customers in the ORDER_HEADER table, as shown in Figure 5-11.

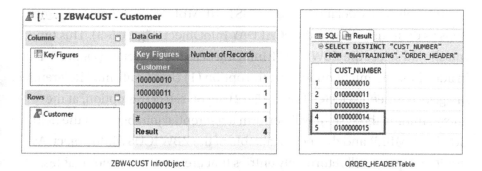

Figure 5-11. Comparison of customer numbers between the
ZBW4CUST InfoObject and the ORDER_HEADER table

As presented in Figure 5-11, the InfoObject ZBW4CUST contains
three Customer values, while in the ORDER_HEADER table there are
five customer numbers available. The highlighted customer numbers
(0100000014 and 0100000015) are not part of the ZBW4CUST master
data. To check how this inconsistency impacts the data model, let's apply
an association between the CUST_NUMBER field and the ZBW4CUST
InfoObject (Figure 5-12).

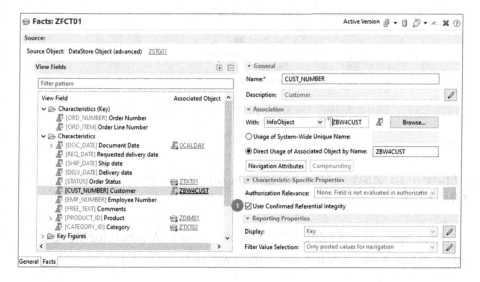

Figure 5-12. Association for Customer field in ZFCT01 Open ODS View

To apply an association for the CUST_NUMBER field, follow the same steps as demonstrated for the 0CALDAY InfoObject (Figure 5-3). This time you should select the ZBW4CUST InfoObject as the reference (Figure 5-10). In addition, you might notice that the option (1) User Confirmed Referential Integrity has been selected (Figure 5-12). If you select this option, at the query runtime the system will perform a referential join between the field CUST_NUMBER and the technical table of the ZBW4CUST InfoObject. As a result, the query will return only entries that are common in both tables.

After applying the association, we can now take advantage of navigation attributes. Follow the steps shown in Figure 5-4 to enable the navigation attributes of the ZBW4CUST InfoObject. Figure 5-13 shows the navigation attributes that were enabled for the ZFCT01 Open ODS View.

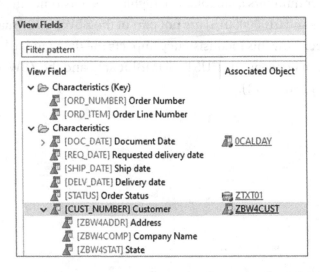

Figure 5-13 *ZBW4CUST navigation attributes in the ZFCT01 Open ODS View*

Let's now open the ZFCT01 Open ODS View in Analysis for Microsoft Excel to check whether the association works as expected.

The Importance of the Referential Integrity Setting

When opening the preview of the ZCPFCT01 Open ODS View in Analysis for Microsoft Excel, by default it shows only the totals. For the given Open ODS View, the Total value of Quantity Ordered is 462 (Figure 5-14).

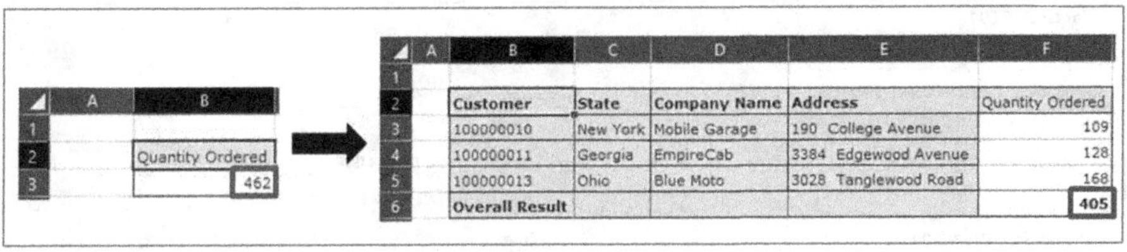

Figure 5-14. *Display of ZBW4CUST attributes for ZCPFCT01 in Analysis for Microsoft Excel (referential integrity option selected)*

On the right side of Figure 5-14, you can see the display after pulling all the customer-related attributes. At first glance, it looks like everything works as expected and the customer-related information is displayed properly. However, you might notice that once the customer information is added to the output, the total value for Quantity Ordered is not 462 but 405. You may also realize that in the underlying ORDER_HEADER table there were five customers available, while the report output shows only three. This behavior is caused by the User Confirmed Referential Integrity option, which we selected when associating the ZBW4CUST InfoObject to the CUST_NUMBER field (Figure 5-12). With this option, every time the associated InfoObject or its navigation attribute is added to the output, the referential join is performed, and it filters out all the records that are not part of the master data of the associated InfoObject. This can cause confusion for the user, because depending on fields that are added to the output, we might see different results. This means that the User Confirmed Referential Integrity property (Figure 5-12) should be used only if we know that referential integrity is ensured. In other words, we need to make sure

that the master data of the associated InfoObject will cover all the values
that are coming from the source table.

Since in our scenario the Customer values that are coming from the
external ORDER_HEADER table are not fully covered by the Customer
master data, let's now unselect the User Confirmed Referential Integrity
property and activate the Open ODS View again (Figure 5-15).

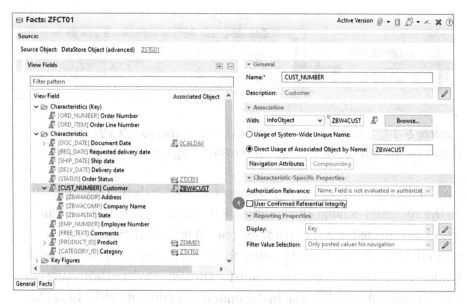

Figure 5-15. *Unselecting the Referential Integrity option for the
Customer field in the ZFCT01 Open ODS View*

After activating the Open ODS View, we can check the output again by
running it in Analysis for Microsoft Excel (Figure 5-16).

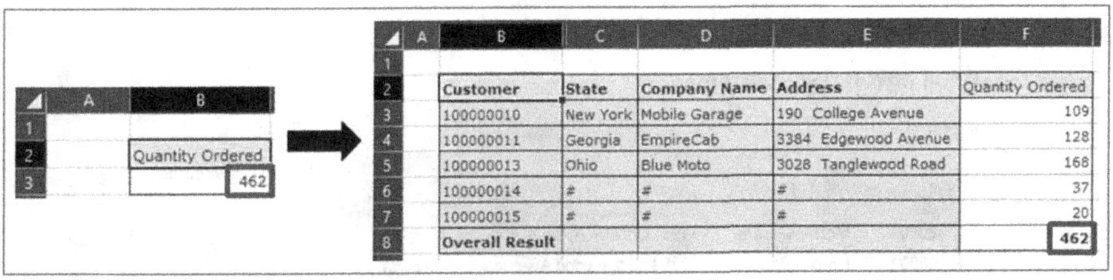

Figure 5-16. *Display of the ZBW4CUST attributes for ZCPFCT01 in Analysis for Microsoft Excel (referential integrity option unselected)*

As shown in Figure 5-16, after we changed the referential integrity option, the customer numbers 0100000014 and 0100000015 are now available. Since the master data for these two customers is not maintained in the ZBW4CUST InfoObject, the attributes State, Company Name, and Address are blank. What is more, the value of Quantity Ordered is now consistent.

Note   When using the User Confirmed Referential Integrity property, you should be aware that at query runtime all values that were not found as part of the master data of the associated InfoObject will be inserted into the master data table of that InfoObject.

As highlighted, you need to be careful when unselecting the User Confirmed Referential Integrity option because this might impact the master data table of the associated InfoObject. Every time you run the preview on the object with associations, the system will propagate the values that are not available in the master data table of the associated InfoObjects. To visualize that, let's check the before and after images of the ZBW4CUST master data table.

Figure 5-17 shows how the content of the ZBW4CUST master data table has changed after we unselect the Referential Integrity option and run the ZCPFCT01 Open ODS View (Figure 5-15).

Before image

⚓ [   ] ZBW4CUST - Customer

Data Grid

| | | | Key Figures | Number of Records |
Customer	Company Name	Address	State	
100000010	Mobile Garage	190 College Avenue	New York	1
100000011	EmpireCab	3384 Edgewood Avenue	Georgia	1
100000013	Blue Moto	3028 Tanglewood Road	Ohio	1
#	#	#	#	1
Result	Result	Result	Result	4

After image

⚓ [   ] ZBW4CUST - Customer

Data Grid

| | | | Key Figures | Number of Records |
Customer	Company Name	State	Address	
100000010	Mobile Garage	New York	190 College Avenue	1
100000011	EmpireCab	Georgia	3384 Edgewood Avenue	1
100000013	Blue Moto	Ohio	3028 Tanglewood Road	1
100000014	#	#	#	1
100000015	#	#	#	1
#	#	#	#	1
Result	Result	Result	Result	6

Figure 5-17. *The ZBW4CUST master data table before and after the ZCPFCT01 Open ODS View execution*

The new entries that are highlighted (0100000014 and 0100000015) were populated into that InfoObject at the Open ODS View's runtime. This means that every time new customer values appear in the underlying ORDER_HEADER table, once the preview on the Open ODS View is executed, they will be added to the master data of the ZBW4CUST InfoObject. Keeping this in mind, you need to be careful when associating fields with InfoObjects, because you might unconsciously propagate master data values that are unwanted. If you want to prevent this situation, you can create a copy of an existing InfoObject and use it instead of the main InfoObject. This is why in some scenarios you might prefer to use the Referential Integrity setting to make sure that the master data will not be messed up.

Since the Open ODS View for the orders data (ZCPFCT01) was updated with new fields, we now need to incorporate these changes within CompositeProvider and Query. First we should update the CompositeProvider object (Figure 5-18).

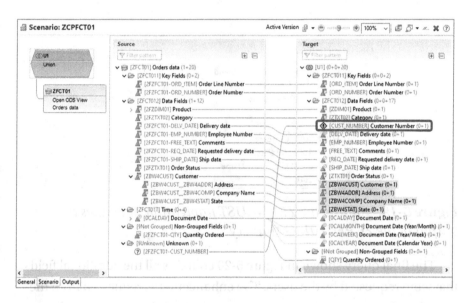

Figure 5-18. *Adding ZBW4CUST navigation attributes to the output of the ZCPFCT01 CompositeProvider*

To display navigation attributes, we should enable them by using the option shown in Figure 5-6. Therefore, we will be able to use customer attributes and map them to the output. As shown in Figure 5-18, we need also to remove the mapping for the CUST_NUMBER field, since the customer's technical name is now inherited from the InfoObject ZBW4CUST. Once we successfully activate the CompositeProvider, as a last step we should update the final query.

Since we removed the CUST_NUMBER field from the underlying CompositeProvider, we need to also remove it from the query. Then we can add new customer-related fields and save the query (Figure 5-19).

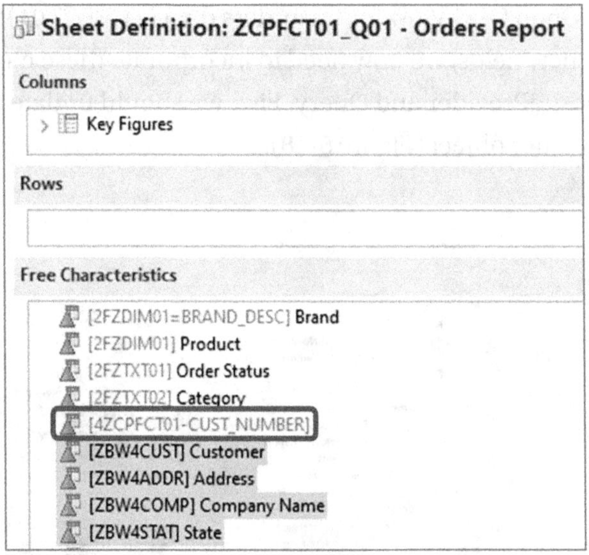

***Figure 5-19.** Adding the ZBW4CUST navigation attributes to the output of the ZCPFCT01_Q01 query*

The final query shown in Figure 5-20 contains all the additional fields that were requested by the users. The enhancements requested from the users have now been implemented.

Order Number	Document Date	Document Date (Calendar Year)	Document Date (Year/Month)	Document Date (Year/Week)	Customer	Address	Company Name	State	Quantity Ordered
0000000001	17.08.2004	2004	08.2004	34.2004	100000010	190 College Avenue	Mobile Garage	New York	55
0000000002	19.08.2004	2004	08.2004	34.2004	100000011	3384 Edgewood Avenue	EmpireCab	Georgia	34
0000000003	20.08.2004	2004	08.2004	34.2004	100000011	3384 Edgewood Avenue	EmpireCab	Georgia	25
0000000004	20.08.2004	2004	08.2004	34.2004	100000013	3028 Tanglewood Road	Blue Moto	Ohio	30
0000000005	21.08.2004	2004	08.2004	34.2004	100000013	3028 Tanglewood Road	Blue Moto	Ohio	6
0000000006	27.08.2004	2004	08.2004	35.2004	100000013	3028 Tanglewood Road	Blue Moto	Ohio	118
0000000007	28.08.2004	2004	08.2004	35.2004	100000010	190 College Avenue	Mobile Garage	New York	1
0000000008	30.08.2004	2004	08.2004	36.2004	100000013	3028 Tanglewood Road	Blue Moto	Ohio	2
0000000009	01.09.2004	2004	09.2004	36.2004	100000013	3028 Tanglewood Road	Blue Moto	Ohio	5
0000000010	03.09.2004	2004	09.2004	36.2004	100000013	3028 Tanglewood Road	Blue Moto	Ohio	7
0000000011	07.09.2004	2004	09.2004	37.2004	100000014	#	#	#	18
0000000012	08.09.2004	2004	09.2004	37.2004	100000015	#	#	#	20
0000000013	08.09.2004	2004	09.2004	37.2004	100000014	#	#	#	11
0000000014	09.09.2004	2004	09.2004	37.2004	100000014	#	#	#	1
0000000015	10.09.2004	2004	09.2004	37.2004	100000010	190 College Avenue	Mobile Garage	New York	43
0000000016	10.09.2004	2004	09.2004	37.2004	100000010	190 College Avenue	Mobile Garage	New York	10
0000000017	15.09.2004	2004	09.2004	38.2004	100000011	3384 Edgewood Avenue	EmpireCab	Georgia	17
0000000018	16.09.2004	2004	09.2004	38.2004	100000011	3384 Edgewood Avenue	EmpireCab	Georgia	23
0000000019	27.09.2004	2004	09.2004	40.2004	100000011	3384 Edgewood Avenue	EmpireCab	Georgia	29
0000000020	30.09.2004	2004	09.2004	40.2004	100000014	#	#	#	7
Overall Result									**462**

***Figure 5-20.** Output of ZCPFCT01_Q01 query in Analysis for Microsoft Excel*

Summary

This chapter demonstrated how we can consume InfoObjects within the models created on top of external sources. We explained how to make associations between fields and InfoObjects. We learned that associations can be applied both at the Open ODS View level and at the CompositeProvider level.

The biggest advantage of hybrid data models is the fact that we can utilize existing master data objects and their functionalities such as hierarchies, navigation attributes, and texts. On the other hand, it was highlighted that hybrid data models can be used only when external attributes are in line with SAP data types and master data content. Otherwise, associations between external fields and InfoObjects may generate the wrong results or cause errors during the reporting.

Finally, we learned the impact of Referential Integrity property. The examples explained the importance of using this setting in a right way and highlighted why it should be used with caution.

CHAPTER 6

Integrating SAP and Non-SAP Data into a Single Data Model

This chapter will walk you through the scenario of implementing a new data model that combines SAP data and non-SAP data. The approach presented in this chapter will use BW/4HANA virtualization capabilities to combine two data models with different structures. In this chapter, you will learn how to integrate SAP and non-SAP models by utilizing the best from both the BW/4HANA and HANA worlds. By using the LSA++ architecture, we will get the benefits of virtual objects to avoid data redundancy and to make the architecture as lean and simple as possible.

Scenario

To create a comprehensive report that gives detailed information about all the orders across the company, business users requested the implementation of a new data model. This data model should include both the SAP and non-SAP information to provide a 360-degree view on

© Konrad Załęski 2021
K. Załęski, *Data Modeling with SAP BW/4HANA 2.0*,
https://doi.org/10.1007/978-1-4842-7089-9_6

the Orders data model. These are the two main SAP objects that should be considered in that model:

- *ZMATID (Material ID)*: This is an InfoObject that covers the SAP Materials master data. The Material ID InfoObject consists of these three attributes:

    - *0CREATEDON (Creation Date)*: Creation date of the material

    - *0NETPRICE (Net Price)*: Net price of the material

    - *0LOC_CURRENCY (Local Currency)*: Net price in the local currency

    Figure 6-1 presents the content and attributes of the ZMATID Material InfoObject.

Material ID		Creation Date	Local Currency		Net Price
11131816	Airbag sensors	01.01.2001	EUR	Euro	130.00 EUR
11138516	Oil level sensor	01.01.2001	EUR	Euro	60.00 EUR
11138529	Coolant temperature sensor	01.03.2003	EUR	Euro	75.00 EUR
41001540	Light sensor	11.05.2003	EUR	Euro	65.00 EUR
46001607	Fuel level sensor	01.01.2001	EUR	Euro	70.00 EUR
#	Not assigned	#	#	Not assigned	0.00

Figure 6-1. *Content of the Material ID InfoObject*

- *ZADS01 (SAP Orders data)*: Advanced DSO that stores SAP orders data. It consists of the following fields:

    - *ZORDID (Order ID)*: Order number

    - *ZORDITM (Order Item)*: Order item number

    - *ZMATID (Material ID)*: Material master data

    - *ZSTORID (Storage Location)*: Storage location of the material

    - *ZBW4CUST (Customer)*: Customer number

- *0DOC_DATE (Document Date)*: Date of the document

- *0SHIP_DATE (Shipping Date)*: Shipping date of the order

- *0ORDER_QUAN (Purchase Order Quantity)*: Ordered quantity

- *0PO_UNIT (Order unit)*: Unit of the ordered quantity

Figure 6-2 presents the content of the ZADS01 (SAP Orders data) ADSO.

Order ID	Order Item	Customer	Material ID		Document Date	Shipping Date	Storage Location	Order quantity
4500000490	10	100000010	46001607	Fuel level sensor	27.12.2009	03.01.2010	2000	6,000 EA
4500000491	10	100000011	11131816	Airbag sensors	31.12.2009	10.01.2010	1000	8,850 EA
4500000492	10	100000011	11138516	Oil level sensor	21.12.2009	21.12.2009	1000	150 EA
4500000493	10	100000010	41001540	Light sensor	07.01.2010	24.01.2010	2000	15,000 EA
4500000494	10	100000011	11138529	Coolant temperature sensor	21.12.2009	21.12.2009	1000	12 EA
4500000494	20	100000011	11138529	Coolant temperature sensor	21.12.2009	21.12.2009	1000	138 EA

Figure 6-2. *Content of SAP Orders ADSO*

As you probably remember, in the external Orders data model we can also distinguish tables with transactional data for Orders (tables ORDERS_HEADER and ORDER_DETAILS) and master data for Products (table PRODUCTS). Figure 6-3 shows the general approach to fulfill the business requirements.

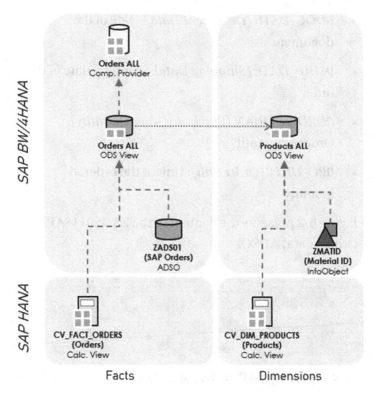

Figure 6-3. *High-level architecture for integrating the SAP and non-SAP Orders data models*

As shown in Figure 6-3, for non-SAP data we will utilize two calculation views. For Orders, we will use the CV_FACT_ORDERS view, which combines the ORDERS_HEADER and ORDERS_DETAILS external tables (see Figure 4-14 in Chapter 4 as a reference). Materials information that is coming from an external system will be derived from the CV_DIM_PRODUCTS view (see Figure 4-4 in Chapter 4 as a reference). SAP-related data will be retrieved from ADSO ZADS01 (SAP Orders) and InfoObject ZMATID (SAP Materials). Our goal is to combine these objects to create a single Facts Open ODS View object for the transactional Orders data and a single Master Data Open ODS View for Materials.

Integrate the Product Master Data into a Single Calculation View

To combine the SAP and non-SAP Materials master data, we will use the HANA layer. While Figure 6-3 showed the high-level architecture for integrating both models, Figure 6-4 is an extension of that architecture and presents the detailed approach for combining the Materials/Products master data into a single dimension.

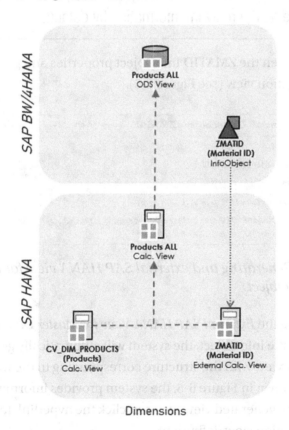

Figure 6-4. *Architecture for integrating SAP and non-SAP Products master data*

In the previous chapter, we created the calculation view for the PRODUCTS table (see Figure 4-4 as a reference), and we will reuse it now. In addition, we need to bring the SAP Materials master data to the HANA layer. This can be achieved by using the functionality of generating external SAP HANA views from InfoObjects.

Note   Instead of using external calculation views, we could query the InfoObject technical tables directly. However, external calculation views provide all the relevant information by default.

Let's now open the ZMATID InfoObject properties and generate an external calculation view (see Figure 6-5).

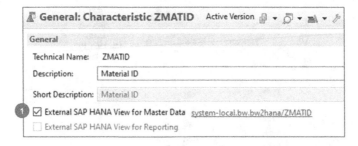

Figure 6-5. *Generating and external SAP HANA view for the ZMATID InfoObject*

By selecting the *External SAP HANA View for Master Data* check box and activating the InfoObject, the system will automatically generate the calculation view with the structure corresponding to the InfoObject structure. As shown in Figure 6-5, the system provides information about a location of the generated view. You can click the hyperlink to open the external calculation view definition.

The generated calculation view contains all the InfoObject attributes as well as the texts columns (Figure 6-6). As discussed in the first chapter, to query data from that calculation view, you need to have authorization for the role that was also generated for that view. For more details about authorization, please refer to Chapter 1.

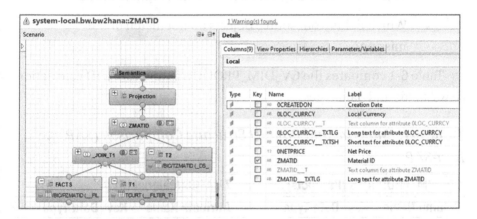

Figure 6-6. *Definition of the external SAP HANA view for the ZMATID InfoObject*

When running a preview for that calculation view, you will see the content data of the Material (ZMATID) InfoObject (see Figure 6-7).

ZMATID	ZMATID__T	ZMATID__TXTLG	0CREATEDON	0NETPRICE	0LOC_CURRCY	0LOC_CURR
00000000011131816	Airbag sensors	Airbag sensors	20010101	130	EUR	?
00000000011138516	Oil level sensor	Oil level sensor	20010101	60	EUR	?
00000000011138529	Coolant temperature sensor	Coolant temperature s...	20030301	75	EUR	?
00000000041001540	Light sensor	Light sensor	20030511	65	EUR	?
00000000046001607	Fuel level sensor	Fuel level sensor	20010101	70	EUR	?
?	?	?	00000000	0		?

Figure 6-7. *Output of the external SAP HANA view for the ZMATID InfoObject*

To properly combine different master data objects, we should first perform the analysis to check the differences in their structure and data types. Based on this analysis, we should identify the following:

- How do we map source fields into the target?

- What should the target data type of the output fields be?

- Which fields from source objects do not match or are missing?

Table 6-1 compares the CV_DIM_PRODUCTS and ZMATID calculation views' fields and data types.

Table 6-1. *Material and Product Structure Comparison (SAP vs. Non-SAP)*

CV_DIM_PRODUCTS (Products)				ZMATID (Material ID)		
Column Name	Key	Data Type		Attribute Name	Key	Data Type
PRODUCT_ID	**X**	VARCHAR(10)	↔	ZMATID	**X**	NVACHAR(18)
CATEGORY_ID	**X**	VARCHAR(5)	↔	**N/A**		
PRODUCT_DESC		VARCHAR(200)	↔	ZMATID___TXTLG		NVARCHAR(60)
BRAND_DESC		VARCHAR(200)	↔	**N/A**		
PRICE		DECIMAL(10,2)	↔	0NETPRICE		DECIMAL(17,2)
CURRENCY		VARCHAR(3)	↔	0LOC_CURRCY		NVARCHAR(5)
N/A			↔	0CREATEDON		NVARCHAR(8)

As presented in Table 6-1, there are four common fields that contain the same information: Product Number, Product Description, Price, and Currency. The remaining three (Category, Brand, and Creation Date) are not common and hence will be available only either for SAP or for non-SAP Materials. An additional difficulty is the fact that the non-SAP dimension has a compounded key based on PRODUCT_ID (Product ID) and CATEGORY_ID (Category ID), while the SAP master data object key consists only of the ZMATID (Material ID) field.

As a next step, we need to indicate the target structure of the consolidated Product Master Data View object. The final Master Data View object should contain not only fields that are common, but also those that are available in only one of these sources. For common fields, it is important to choose the right data type that will cover the values from both sources. If we do not set the right data type, some values might be wrongly displayed (i.e., truncated), or the view will return an error during activation. Based on Table 6-1, we can easily define the target data type for each output field. If we are considering fields that are common in both data sources, then we should always choose the data type with the greater length to make sure that the values will not be truncated. Table 6-2 lists the target structure and data types for the consolidated Product calculation view.

Table 6-2. *Target Data Types for Combined Product Calculation View*

CV_DIM_PRODUCTS_ALL (Products ALL)		
Column Name	Key	Data Type
PRODUCT_ID	X	NVACHAR(18)
CATEGORY_ID	X	NVARCHAR(5)
PRODUCT_DESC		NVARCHAR(200)
BRAND_DESC		NVARCHAR(200)
NET_PRICE		DECIMAL(17,2)
CURRENCY		NVARCHAR(5)
CREATED_ON		NVARCHAR(8)

As we have identified the target structure of our view, we can now start to create a consolidated calculation view. First, we need switch to the *SAP HANA modeler* perspective. Then, in the target package, we should create a new calculation view of the DIMENSION type. As we will query the data from two calculation views, we need to add two projections by dragging them from the editor's palette. Then as the source for projections we should select the ZMATID calculation view for the SAP master data and the CV_DIM_PRODUCTS calculation view for non-SAP data (Figure 6-8).

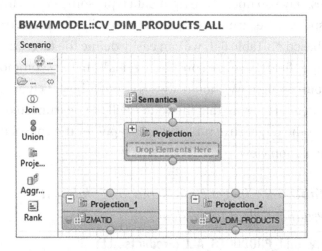

Figure 6-8. *Adding data sources to the CV_DIM_PRODUCTS_ALL calculation view*

For each Projection node, we should select the fields that we will use for mapping. As per Table 6-1 for the ZMATID calculation view we will use five fields, which should be selected (Figure 6-9).

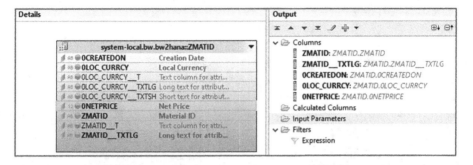

Figure 6-9. *Adding the ZMATID fields to the output of the Projection node in the CV_DIM_PRODUCTS_ALL calculation view*

For the projection that queries data from the CV_DIM_PRODUCTS calculation view, we will add all the available fields to the output of the node (Figure 6-10).

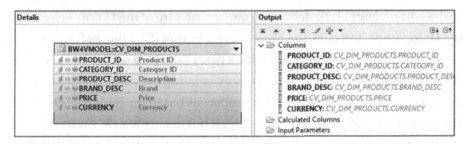

Figure 6-10. *Adding CV_DIM_PRODUCTS fields to the output of the Projection node in the CV_DIM_PRODUCTS_ALL calculation view*

Next we need to combine data from both Projection nodes into the single dataset. For that purpose, we will use the Union node. After adding the Union node from the palette, we need to create a target structure that will be used for mapping fields from the underlying projections. We will use Table 6-2 as a reference for creating the target structure and assigning the right data types in the Union node. Figure 6-11 presents the steps for defining the target structure of the Union node.

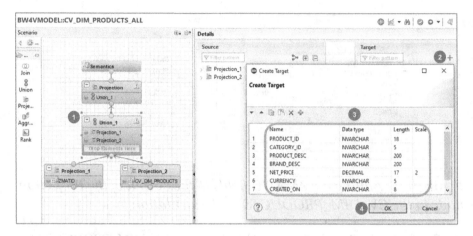

Figure 6-11. *Defining the target structure of the Union node in the CV_DIM_PRODUCTS_ALL calculation view*

To add the Union node, you can drag the Union icon from the palette to the editor view (1). To define the target structure of the Union, select the Union node and click the *Create Target* button (2). Then define the target fields and assign the proper data types (3). Since we performed the analysis of the target structure before creating the view, now we can easily define all the fields and their properties based on Table 6-2. Once the structure is defined, we can confirm it by clicking the *OK* button (4). With this activity we created a target structure of the consolidated Products dimension. Now we need to map fields from the underlying projections to the target structure. Figure 6-12 shows the target mapping for the Union node.

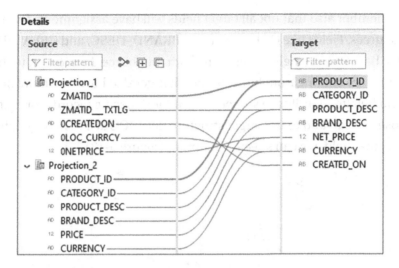

Figure 6-12. *Defining the fields mapping for the Union node in the CV_DIM_PRODUCTS_ALL calculation view*

To properly map the source fields to targets, we can use Table 6-1 as a reference. To map the source field into the target, we can simply drag and drop them.

Important   When defining associations, you should always start the mapping from the source field that is of the same data type as the target field. Otherwise, the system will inherit the data type from the field that was mapped as the first one and overwrite our initial settings.

As mentioned, we should start the mapping always from the field with the "leading" data type. As an example for the PRODUCT_ID target field, we should first map the field ZMATID from *Projection_1* and then map the PRODUCT_ID field from *Projection_2*. If we map PRODUCT_ID from *Projection_2* first, then the target PRODUCT_ID will inherit the data type from that field, which is VARCHAR(10) instead of VARCHAR(18).

Remember also that not all target fields will have assignments from both sources. Fields like CATEGORY_ID, BRAND_DESC, and CREATED_ON will have only a single assignment from the source. In addition to the fields that are coming from both sources, it is good to have one more field that will help to identify the source system for a specific record. For that purpose, we can add to the target structure field SOURCE. Then by right-clicking that field, we can specify mappings (Figure 6-13).

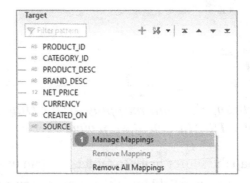

Figure 6-13. *Adding the SOURCE field to the Union node in the CV_DIM_PRODUCTS_ALL calculation view*

Once the *Manage Mappings* option is selected, the window for defining the mapping will pop up. Here we can define constant values for the underlying sources.

As shown in Figure 6-14, when managing the mapping, we can specify constant values for each projection that is connected to the Union node. For *Projection_1,* which points to the ZMATID data, we can specify SAP as a constant value. *Projection_2* queries data from the external Product dimension; hence, I assigned EXT as a constant value. It is useful to add such a column to the output structure, since it will allow users to easily identify or filter records only from specific system (but it is not mandatory).

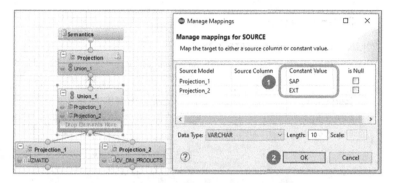

Figure 6-14. *"Manage mappings for SOURCE" fields in the CV_
DIM_PRODUCTS_ALL calculation view*

We can use the manage mappings functionality also to assign constant
values, in case mapping is not maintained for some Projection nodes. By
default when there is no mapping from the underlying node, the output
column will display NULLs for this data. In our scenario, this is a case
for the CATEGORY_ID column. Since CATEGORY_ID will be part of the
primary key of the target Product dimension, we need to ensure that there
will be no NULL values there. To achieve that, we should replace NULLs
with the constant values for that field. To apply a fixed value, right-click the
CATEGORY_ID field and select the *Manage Mappings* option to open the
window for defining the mappings (Figure 6-15).

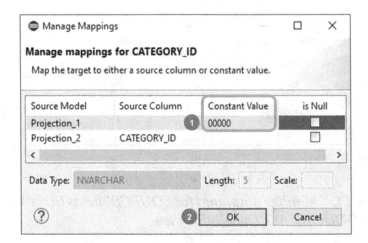

Figure 6-15. *Managing the mappings for the CATEGORY_ID field in the CV_DIM_PRODUCTS_ALL calculation view*

As shown in Figure 6-15, for the target CATEGORY_ID field, I assigned a value of 00000 for the data coming from *Projection_1* (SAP Materials). After applying the mapping, CATEGORY_ID values will always show 00000 instead of NULL for the SAP Materials master data. For external data, Category values will be populated from the *Projection_2* node.

Once we have configured the final structure on the Union node level, we can then go to the final Projection node and add all the fields to the output of the view (Figure 6-16).

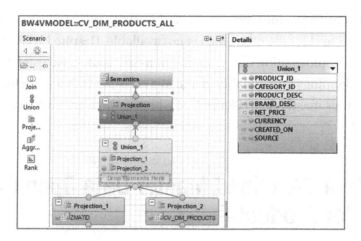

Figure 6-16. *Adding fields to the output of the CV_DIM_PRODUCTS_ALL calculation view*

After defining the final output of CV_DIM_PRODUCTS_ALL, we can activate the view. Then run the data preview to validate the content (Figure 6-17).

PRODUCT_ID	CATEGORY_ID	PRODUCT_DESC	BRAND_DESC	NET_PRICE	CURRENCY	CREATED_ON	SOURCE
00000000011131816	00000	Airbag sensors	?	130	EUR	20010101	SAP
00000000011138516	00000	Oil level sensor	?	60	EUR	20010101	SAP
00000000011138529	00000	Coolant temperature s...	?	75	EUR	20030301	SAP
00000000041001540	00000	Light sensor	?	65	EUR	20030511	SAP
00000000046001607	00000	Fuel level sensor	?	70	EUR	20010101	SAP
	00000	?	?	0		00000000	SAP
AC001	0001	A/C Gas Receiver	AUTOprism	70	USD	?	EXT
AC002	0001	A/C Condenser Filter	AUTOprism	150	USD	?	EXT
AC003	0001	A/C Cabin Filter	AUTOprism	30	USD	?	EXT
AV001	0002	Radio and media player	Fly Audio	120	USD	?	EXT

Figure 6-17. *Data preview of the CV_DIM_PRODUCTS_ALL calculation view*

The data preview returns the combined view for the Products master data. The SOURCE column clearly helps us to identify the source system for a specific set of records. You can also notice that the BRAND_DESC and CREATED_ON columns display question marks for specific sets of data. Question marks represent NULL values, meaning that there is no data available. This is because these two columns have assignment to only one data source, and for the other, data is not available. Despite CATEGORY_ID retrieving information only from the non-SAP source, we used the Manage Mappings functionality to assign a constant 00000 value for the SAP Materials master data (Figure 6-15); hence, there are no NULL values displayed.

Create a Combined Master Data Open ODS View for Products

In the previous section, we consolidated the SAP and non-SAP master data for Products into the single calculation view. As per our architecture design (Figure 6-4), on top of this view (CV_DIM_PRODUCTS_ALL) we should now create the BW/4 Master Data object. Let's now create the consolidated Master Data Open ODS View object named Product.

Figure 6-18 shows the initial setup for the consolidated Master Data Open ODS View for Products. The Representative Key Field is set to the PRODUCT_ID column (1). In addition, the column CATEGORY_ID is also part of the primary key; hence, it was added to the Characteristics (Key) section (2). BRAN_DESC, CREATED_ON, and SOURCE are attributes and were added to the Characteristics section (3). NET_PRICE is a measure, so it's assigned to the Key Figures folder (4), while for the CURRENCY column there is a dedicated Currency section (5). The PRODUCT_DESC field contains product descriptions, and it's added to the Long Text section (6).

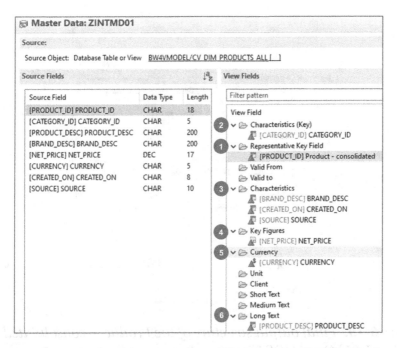

Figure 6-18. *Initial output structure of Product—consolidated (ZINTMD01) Open ODS View object*

After configuring the initial structure of the consolidated Product dimension, now we should apply additional adjustments. Figure 6-19 shows the final structure of the integrated Product dimension.

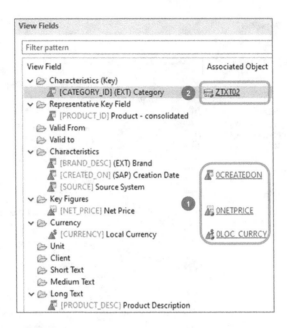

Figure 6-19. *Final output structure of the Product—consolidated (ZINTMD01) Open ODS View*

First, we can identify the fields for which we can apply associations. The fields CREATED_ON, NET_PRICE, and CURRENCY can be associated with the 0CREATEDON, 0NETPRICE, and 0LOC_CURRCY InfoObjects accordingly (1). Remember that when you assign the 0LOC_CURRCY InfoObject, you need to make sure that the external table will always return SAP-specific currency values.

Important   If you created a Master Data Open ODS View with a compounded key, meaning that you assigned fields to the Characteristics (Key) section, each of those field needs to have an association set. In addition, the option Direct Usage of Associated Object by Name needs to be selected when applying associations.

As mentioned for fields assigned to the *Characteristics (Key)* section, we need to apply direct associations. Otherwise, we will not be able to utilize that Open ODS View for associations, which is required in our scenario. Having said that, we need to configure the association for CATEGORY_ID. In previous chapters, we created the Text ZTXT02 Open ODS View object for Category (Figure 4-7). I can use this object to apply a direct association between the CATEGORY_ID field and the ZTXT02 Open ODS View object (2).

Finally, we should apply adjustments for the field descriptions. For fields that are available for only a specific system, it is good to include such information in the header. This is why in the field descriptions, I added a leading EXT prefix (which stands for External) for CATEGORY_ID and BRAND_DESC and a leading SAP prefix for the CREATED_ON field. Thanks to that, in the front-end tool it will be easy to identify all the fields that are relevant for one or the other system. To check the final result of our consolidated Product dimension, I will open the preview of the ZINTMD01 Open ODS View object in the Analysis for Microsoft Excel tool.

Figure 6-20 presents the output of the combined Product dimension. The SAP and non-SAP master data is now consolidated into the single dataset. The Source System column helps to immediately identify or filter products either from SAP or from the external system. Column headers indicate whether a column is specific only for the external system (the EXT prefix in the column header), SAP system (the SAP prefix in the column header), or data coming from both systems (no prefix in the column header).

Product - consolidated		(EXT) Category	Source System	(EXT) Brand	(SAP) Creation Date	Net Price
00000/#	00000/Not assigned	00000	SAP	#	#	0.00
0001/AC003	A/C Cabin Filter	Air conditioning system (A/C)	EXT	AUTOprism	#	$ 30.00
0001/AC002	A/C Condenser Filter	Air conditioning system (A/C)	EXT	AUTOprism	#	$ 150.00
0001/AC001	A/C Gas Receiver	Air conditioning system (A/C)	EXT	AUTOprism	#	$ 70.00
00000/00000000011131816	Airbag sensors	00000	SAP	#	01.01.2001	130.00 EUR
0002/AV004	Antenna	Audio/video devices	EXT	Fly Audio	#	$ 30.00
0003/CS001	Arm Rest	Car seat	EXT	Exclusive Car Interior	#	$ 65.00
0003/CS002	Bucket seat	Car seat	EXT	Exclusive Car Interior	#	$ 465.00
0003/CS003	Children and baby car seat	Car seat	EXT	Exclusive Car Interior	#	$ 170.00
00000/00000000011138529	Coolant temperature sensor	00000	SAP	#	01.03.2003	75.00 EUR
00000/00000000046001607	Fuel level sensor	00000	SAP	#	01.01.2001	70.00 EUR
00000/00000000041001540	Light sensor	00000	SAP	#	11.05.2003	65.00 EUR
00000/00000000011138516	Oil level sensor	00000	SAP	#	01.01.2001	60.00 EUR
0002/AV001	Radio and media player	Audio/video devices	EXT	Fly Audio	#	$ 120.00
0003/CS005	Seat belt	Car seat	EXT	MotoSpec	#	30.00 EUR
0003/CS006	Seat bracket	Car seat	EXT	MotoSpec	#	75.00 EUR
0002/AV002	Speaker	Audio/video devices	EXT	Fly Audio	#	$ 60.00
0002/AV003	Tuner	Audio/video devices	EXT	Fly Audio	#	$ 80.00

Figure 6-20. *Final output of the ZINTMD01 object in Analysis for Microsoft Excel*

Integrate the Orders Fact Data into a Single Calculation View

For the fact data, we will follow the same approach as for the master data integration. This means that integration of transactional data will be also implemented on the HANA layer. Figure 6-21 presents a detailed approach for integrating SAP and non-SAP fact data into a single dataset.

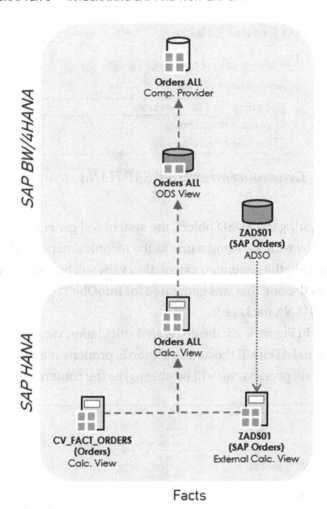

Facts

Figure 6-21. *Architecture for integrating SAP and non-SAP Orders fact data*

The architecture shown in Figure 6-21 is similar to the one that we implemented for the Products master data. The main difference here is that for Facts, we will be generating an external calculation view from an ADSO. For Orders data, we will utilize the transactional CV_FACT_ ORDERS calculation view that was created in Chapter 4 (see Figure 4-14). To generate the calculation view from the ZADS01 ADSO, in the ADSO properties, select the External Calculation View option (Figure 6-22).

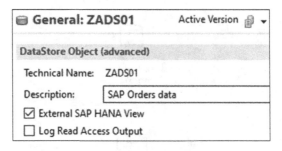

Figure 6-22. *Generating an external SAP HANA view for the ZADS01 ADSO*

After activating the ADSO object, the system will generate the calculation view with the same name as the technical name of the ADSO. By default, the generated calculation view will be located in the same place as the one that was generated for InfoObject (the system-local. bw.bw2hana HANA package).

As shown in Figure 6-23, the generated calculation view contains fields from the original ADSO. If the authorization is properly maintained, after running the data preview, we will be able to see the content of that view.

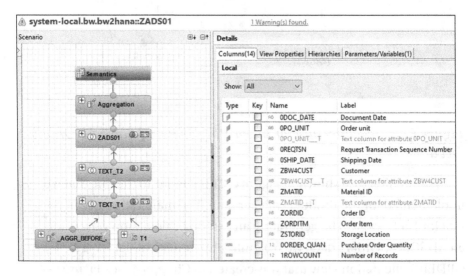

Figure 6-23. *Definition of the external SAP HANA view for the ZADS01 ADSO*

As shown in Figure 6-24, the output of that view corresponds to the content of the source ADSO (see Figure 6-2 as a reference). In the next step, we need to perform an analysis of how to combine the SAP and non-SAP Orders data.

ZORDID	ZORDITM	ODOC_DATE	OSHIP_DATE	ZMATID	ZMATID_T	ZSTORID	OPO_UNIT	ZBW4CUST	OORDER_QUAN
4500000492	000010	20091221	20091221	00000000011138516	Oil level sensor	1000	EA	0100000011	150 EA
4500000494	000010	20091221	20091221	00000000011138529	Coolant tempera...	1000	EA	0100000011	12 EA
4500000491	000010	20091231	20100110	00000000011131816	Airbag sensors	1000	EA	0100000011	8,850 EA
4500000494	000020	20091221	20091221	00000000011138529	Coolant tempera...	1000	EA	0100000011	138 EA
4500000490	000010	20091227	20100103	00000000046001607	Fuel level sensor	2000	EA	0100000010	6,000 EA
4500000493	000010	20100107	20100124	00000000041001540	Light sensor	2000	EA	0100000010	15,000 EA

Figure 6-24. Output of the external SAP HANA view for the ZADS01 ADSO

To start the analysis, let's compare structures of the transactional views. Table 6-3 compares fields and data types of the CV_FACT_ORDERS and ZADS01 calculation views.

Table 6-3. Orders Structure Comparison (SAP vs. Non-SAP)

CV_FACT_ORDERS (Orders)				ZADS01 (SAP Orders)		
Column Name	Key	Data Type		Attribute Name	Key	Data Type
ORD_NUMBER	X	VARCHAR(10)	↔	ZORDID	X	NVACHAR(10)
ORD_ITEM	X	VARCHAR(3)	↔	ZORDITM	X	NVARCHAR(6)
DOC_DATE		DATE	↔	ODOC_DATE		NVARCHAR(8)
REQ_DATE		DATE	↔	N/A		
SHIP_DATE		DATE	↔	OSHIP_DATE		NVARCHAR(8)
DELV_DATE		DATE	↔	**N/A**		
STATUS		VARCHAR(3)	↔	**N/A**		
CUST_NUMBER		VARCHAR(10)	↔	ZBW4CUST		NVARCHAR(10)

(continued)

Table 6-3. (*continued*)

CV_FACT_ORDERS (Orders)				ZADS01 (SAP Orders)		
Column Name	Key	Data Type		Attribute Name	Key	Data Type
EMP_NUMBER		VARCHAR(10)	↔	N/A		
FREE_TEXT		VARCHAR(100)	↔	N/A		
PRODUCT_ID		VARCHAR(10)	↔	ZMATID		NVARCHAR(18)
CATEGORY_ID		VARCHAR(5)	↔	N/A		
QTY		INTEGER	↔	0ORDER_QUAN		DECIMAL(17,2)
N/A			↔	0PO_UNIT		NVARCHAR(3)
N/A			↔	ZSTORID		NVARCHAR(4)

As we already know, based on the comparison, we should identify the target structure and data types for the combined dataset. For common fields, we need to specify the data type that will support both the source column types. Data types for fields that are specific only for single source can be inherited directly from the source column. Table 6-4 presents the target structure and data types for the consolidated Orders view.

Table 6-4. *Target Data Types for Combined Orders Calculation View*

CV_FACT_ORDERS_ALL (Orders ALL)

Column Name	Key	Data Type
ORDER_ID	X	NVACHAR(10)
ORDER_ITEM	X	NVARCHAR(6)
DOC_DATE		DATE
REQ_DATE		DATE
SHIP_DATE		DATE
DELV_DATE		DATE
STATUS		VARCHAR(3)
CUST_NUMBER		NVARCHAR(10)
EMP_NUMBER		VARCHAR(10)
FREE_TEXT		VARCHAR(100)
PRODUCT_ID		NVACHAR(18)
CATEGORY_ID		NVARCHAR(5)
QUANTITY		DECIMAL(17,2)
UNIT		NVARCHAR(3)
STOR_LOC		NVARCHAR(4)

Based on Table 6-4, we can now implement the calculation view for the consolidated Orders data. To start, we should first create a new calculation view of the CUBE type. Then we should add two Projection nodes (for retrieving SAP and non-SAP Orders data) and a Union node for merging the Orders data into a single dataset. As a reference for defining the output structure of the Union node, we can use Table 6-4. Figure 6-25 presents the target structure of the Union node for the transactional CV_FACT_ ORDERS_ALL calculation view.

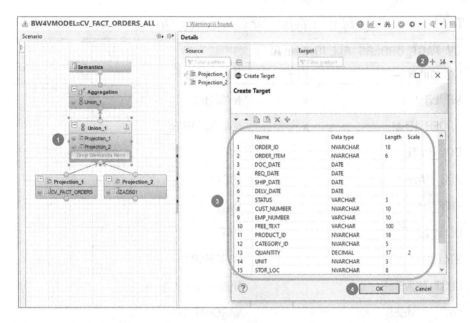

Figure 6-25. *Defining the target structure of the Union node in the CV_FACT_ORDERS_ALL calculation view*

As shown in Figure 6-25, Projection_1 retrieves data from the CV_FACT_ORDERS calculation view, while Projection_2 uses the ZADS01 calculation view as a source. They are linked to the Union node. On the right side of the screen, you can see the target structure of the Union node that was created according to the field definitions in Table 6-4. After creating the structure, we should define the mappings using Table 6-3 as a reference (Figure 6-26).

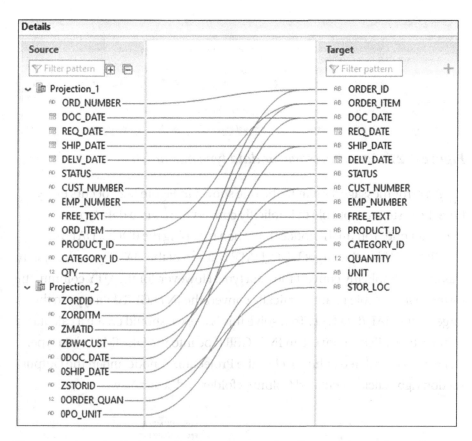

Figure 6-26. *Defining a fields mapping for the Union node in the CV_FACT_ORDERS calculation view*

When defining the mapping, make sure that for each target field, you first map the field with the same data type as the target one. This is because the system will inherit the data type from the column that was mapped as the first one.

After applying the mappings on the Union node level, you can add all the fields to the output of the final Aggregation node and validate the model. Apparently the system will return an error, as in Figure 6-27.

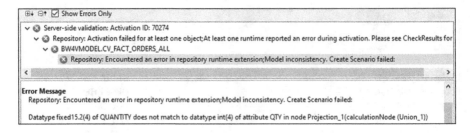

Figure 6-27. *Error message for data type mismatch*

An error message similar to the one shown in Figure 6-27 occurs every time the system is not able to implicitly convert the source data type to the target one. You might notice that when mapping the 0DOC_DATE of NVARCHAR(8) to the target DOC_DATE column of the DATE type, the system was able to implicitly convert the data type. However, for the QTY column, the system was not able to automatically convert the INTEGER data type to the target DECIMAL data type. To resolve this issue, we should create a calculated column to explicitly convert an INTEGER type into the DECIMAL data type. To create a calculated column, click the Projection_1 node and in the Output section right-click Calculated Columns folder and select New.

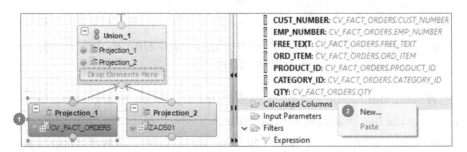

Figure 6-28. *Creating a calculated column for the Quantity field in the CV_FACT_ORDERS_ALL calculation view*

After selecting the New option, the system will open the Calculated Column editor. Here you can specify the column that you want to convert and the target data type.

When creating a calculated column, first you need to provide its name (1). It should be unique, meaning that there should not be any column with the same name already in existence. In my case, I named it CA_QTY (Figure 6-29). Then you need to provide the target column data type (2), which in our case is DECIMAL(17,2). To convert the column to DECIMAL, we do not need to apply any conversion function, but simply provide the name of the column that we want to convert (3). We can click the Validate Syntax button to make sure that the expression is valid, and then we can proceed by clicking the OK button (4).

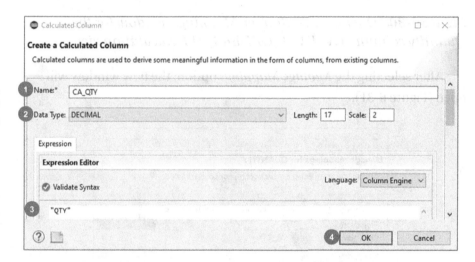

Figure 6-29. *Specifying the definition of the CA_QTY calculated column in the CV_FACT_ORDERS_ALL calculation view*

Once we create the calculated column, we should adjust the mapping in the Union node. We can change the mappings by right-clicking the target column and selecting the *Manage Mappings* option (see Figure 6-30).

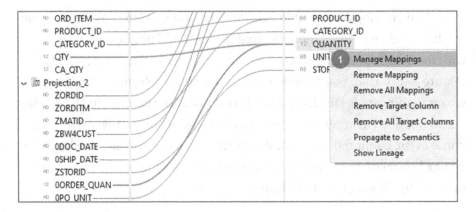

Figure 6-30. *Opening the Manage Mappings window for the Quantity column's CV_FACT_ORDERS_ALL calculation view*

After selecting the *Manage Mappings* option, the new window will open (Figure 6-31).

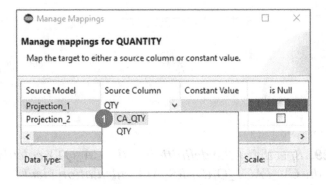

Figure 6-31. *Manage Mappings for Quantity column in the CV_FACT_ORDERS_ALL calculation view*

In the Manage Mappings window, we can replace the QTY column with the newly created CA_QTY calculated column (Figure 6-31). After confirming the mappings, you can validate the view, and the error should not appear anymore.

There are two additional mappings that we should adjust. First, we need to ensure that transactional data will have the same values for the combination of PRODUCT_ID and CATEGORY_ID, which are the primary keys of the consolidated Product dimension. Based on these key field values, we will later apply an association with the Product Open ODS View object; hence, we need to ensure that key values will be matching. This is the reason why we need to replace NULLs with 00000 values for the CATEGORY_ID field, the same as we did in the Product calculation view (follow the same configuration as shown in Figure 6-15).

The second adjustment could be applied for the UNIT column. For non-SAP data, this column is also not maintained, but since in our scenario, the order quantity always refers to the number of items, we can assign EA (each) as a constant value (Figure 6-32).

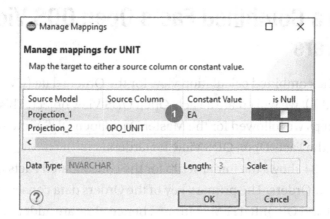

***Figure 6-32.** Manage Mappings for Unit column in the CV_FACT_ ORDERS_ALL calculation view*

By ensuring valid unit values for all the records, we will be able to utilize the UNIT column as the unit element for the Order Quantity key figure at the Open ODS View level. Thanks to that, during reporting, users will be able to see key figure values with the unit assigned. After applying all the adjustments, we can activate the calculation view and run the data preview.

The data preview (Figure 6-33) returns the combined view for the Orders transactional data. Now we can build the Facts Open ODS View object on top of the combined dataset.

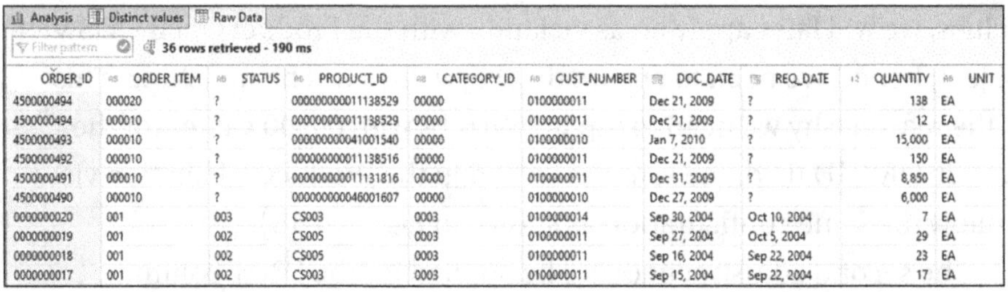

ORDER_ID	ORDER_ITEM	STATUS	PRODUCT_ID	CATEGORY_ID	CUST_NUMBER	DOC_DATE	REQ_DATE	QUANTITY	UNIT
4500000494	000020	?	00000000011138529	00000	0100000011	Dec 21, 2009	?	138	EA
4500000494	000010	?	00000000011138529	00000	0100000011	Dec 21, 2009	?	12	EA
4500000493	000010	?	00000000041001540	00000	0100000010	Jan 7, 2010	?	15,000	EA
4500000492	000010	?	00000000011138516	00000	0100000011	Dec 21, 2009	?	150	EA
4500000491	000010	?	00000000011131816	00000	0100000011	Dec 31, 2009	?	8,850	EA
4500000490	000010	?	00000000046001607	00000	0100000010	Dec 27, 2009	?	6,000	EA
0000000020	001	003	CS003	0003	0100000014	Sep 30, 2004	Oct 10, 2004	7	EA
0000000019	001	002	CS005	0003	0100000011	Sep 27, 2004	Oct 5, 2004	29	EA
0000000018	001	002	CS005	0003	0100000011	Sep 16, 2004	Sep 22, 2004	23	EA
0000000017	001	002	CS003	0003	0100000011	Sep 15, 2004	Sep 22, 2004	17	EA

Figure 6-33. *Data preview of the CV_FACT_ORDERS_ALL calculation view*

Create a Combined Facts Open ODS View for Orders

On top of the combined calculation view for the Orders data (CV_FACT_ORDERS_ALL), we will create a Facts Open ODS View object. This requires the same steps we followed for the Master Data Open ODS View, so let's now create the Facts Open ODS View for Orders.

Figure 6-34 shows the initial setup for the consolidated Facts Open ODS View for Orders. The primary key of the Orders data consists of the ORDER_ID and ORDER_ITEM columns; hence, they are added to the *Characteristics (Key)* section (1). The underlying calculation view contains one measure, which is QUANTITY. This measure is added to the *Key Figures* section (2). The UNIT column goes into the dedicated *Unit* folder (3). The remaining fields are assigned to the *Characteristics* section (4).

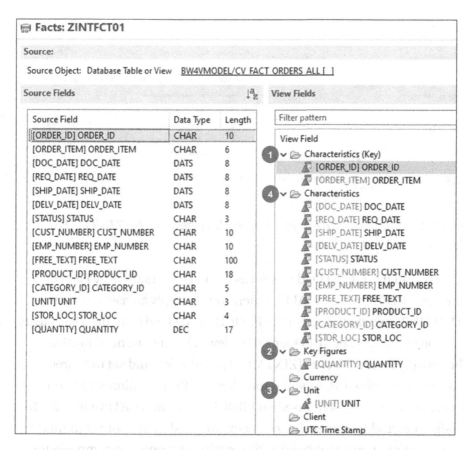

Figure 6-34. *Initial output structure of the consolidated Orders (ZINTFCT01) Open ODS View*

After the initial distribution of fields between specific folders, we can now implement additional enhancements. Our target is to build the star schema model by applying an association with Master Data objects. The main Master Data object in our data model is the Product (ZINTMD01) dimension, which we created in the previous section. Let's now apply an association between the Orders transactional data and the Product dimension (Figure 6-35).

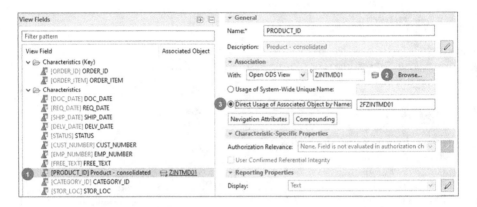

Figure 6-35. *Association for the Product field in the ZINTFCT01 Open ODS View object*

The PRODUCT_ID field was set as the Representative Key Field of the ZINTMD01 Products (ALL) dimension. To apply an association to ZINTMD01, we should select the PRODUCT_ID field from the View Fields section of the ZINTFCT01 Open ODS View (1). Then we need to click Browse (2) for the Product (ZINTMD01) dimension and set the Direct Association option (3). As you remember, the Product dimension consists of the compounding key based on PRODUCT_ID and CATEGORY_ID. To assign the Product dimension correctly, we need to use both columns for the association. As mentioned in the previous section, the compounding keys should always contain the association. This is why when defining the Product dimension, we assigned the ZTXT02 Open ODS View to CATEGORY_ID (Figure 6-19). To complete the association to the Product dimension, we need to first assign the ZTXT02 Open ODS View to the CATEGORY_ID field (Figure 6-36).

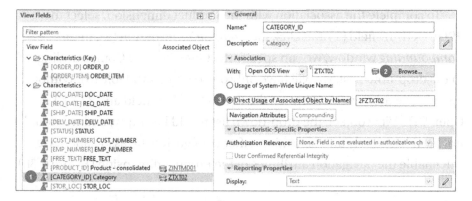

Figure 6-36. *Association for the Category field in the ZINTFCT01 Open ODS View object*

Once we apply an association for the CATEGORY_ID field, we can complete the association with the Product (ZINTMD01) dimension (see Figure 6-37).

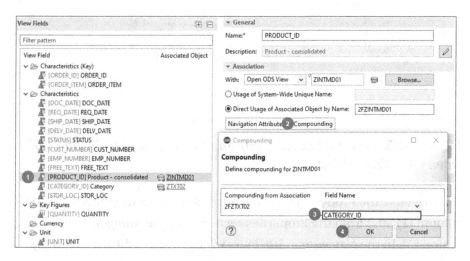

Figure 6-37. *Defining the compounding for the Product field in the ZINTFCT01 Open ODS View object*

To complete the association with the Product dimension, select the PRODUCT_ID field (1) and click the *Compounding* button (2). In the *Compounding* window, we can specify the target field for Compounding. In the drop-down list, we will have only one column available (3). Without applying an association between the CATEGORY_ID field and ZTXT02 Open ODS View object, the drop-down list would be empty, and we would not be able to apply an association. After configuring the association, we can enable the navigation attributes of the Product dimension (Figure 6-38).

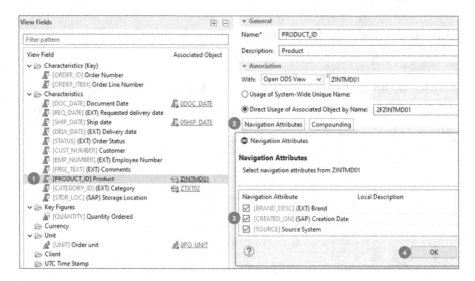

Figure 6-38. *Selecting the navigation attributes for the ZINTFCT01 Open ODS View object*

To enable the Product navigation attributes, select the PRODUCT_ID column (1), and from the Properties section click the *Navigation Attributes* button (2). In the *Navigation Attributes* window, select the attributes (3) and confirm the action by clicking the *OK* button (4).

To complete the configuration of the ZINTFCT01 Open ODS View object, we should adjust the descriptions to make them meaningful to end users. Additionally, we can apply associations for some other fields, as shown in Figure 6-39.

View Fields	
Filter pattern	
View Field	**Associated Object**
∨ 🗁 Characteristics (Key)	
🏛 [ORDER_ID] Order Number	
🏛 [ORDER_ITEM] Order Line Number	
∨ 🗁 Characteristics	
🏛 [DOC_DATE] Document Date	🏛 0DOC_DATE
🏛 [REQ_DATE] (EXT) Requested delivery date	
🏛 [SHIP_DATE] Ship date	🏛 0SHIP_DATE
🏛 [DELV_DATE] (EXT) Delivery date	
🏛 [STATUS] (EXT) Order Status	
🏛 [CUST_NUMBER] Customer	
🏛 [EMP_NUMBER] (EXT) Employee Number	
🏛 [FREE_TEXT] (EXT) Comments	
∨ 🏛 [PRODUCT_ID] Product	📇 ZINTMD01
🏛 [BRAND_DESC] (EXT) Brand	
🏛 [CREATED_ON] (SAP) Creation Date	
🏛 [SOURCE] Source System	
🏛 [CATEGORY_ID] (EXT) Category	📇 ZTXT02
🏛 [STOR_LOC] (SAP) Storage Location	
∨ 🗁 Key Figures	
🏛 [QUANTITY] Quantity Ordered	
🗁 Currency	
∨ 🗁 Unit	
💲 [UNIT] Order unit	💲 0PO_UNIT
🗁 Client	
🗁 UTC Time Stamp	

Figure 6-39. *Final output structure of the Orders (ZINTFCT01) Open ODS View*

As presented in Figure 6-39, the descriptions for all the fields were adjusted. The trailing "EXT" and "SAP" description prefixes enable us to easily identify whether the field is specific only for the external data source or for SAP data only. The fields DOC_DATE, SHIP_DATE, and UNIT were associated with the standard SAP InfoObjects 0DOC_DATE, 0SHIP_DATE, and 0PO_UNIT accordingly.

The last enhancement that will be performed is to set the Unit Element property for the Quantity Ordered key figure (Figure 6-40).

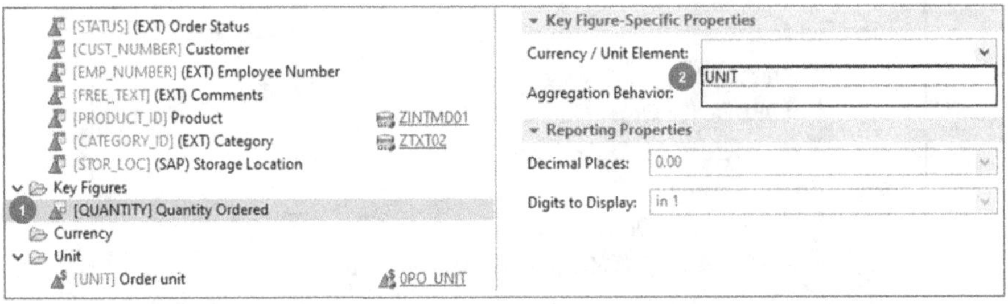

Figure 6-40. *Assigning the Unit element for the Quantity Ordered field in the ZINTFCT01 Open ODS View object*

When opening the properties of the QUANTITY field (1), we can specify the unit element for the measure (2). From the drop-down, we will be able to select the field that was assigned to the *Unit* section. If there is no field in that section, the drop-down list will be empty. After the activation of the ZINTFCT01 Open ODS View object, we can validate the results (Figure 6-41).

Order Number	Order Line Number	Product	Customer	Ship date	(SAP) Storage Location	(EXT) Order Status	Quantity Ordered
0000000001	001	A/C Gas Receiver	0100000010	19.08.2004	#	001	25.00 EA
0000000001	002	A/C Condenser Filter	0100000010	19.08.2004	#	001	30.00 EA
0000000002	001	Antenna	0100000011	23.08.2004	#	001	13.00 EA
0000000002	002	Bucket seat	0100000011	23.08.2004	#	001	2.00 EA
0000000002	003	Seat bracket	0100000011	23.08.2004	#	001	19.00 EA
4500000490	000010	Fuel level sensor	0100000010	03.01.2010	2000	#	6,000.00 EA
4500000494	000010	Coolant temperature sensor	0100000011	21.12.2009	1000	#	12.00 EA
4500000494	000020	Coolant temperature sensor	0100000011	21.12.2009	1000	#	138.00 EA

Figure 6-41. *Final output of the ZINTFCT01 object in Analysis for Microsoft Excel*

As presented in Figure 6-41, the SAP and non-SAP orders are now combined into a single dataset. Thanks to the proper association with the Product dimension, users are able to see the product names instead of the numbers. The prefixes in the column headers help us to understand if the column is SAP or non-SAP-specific. The Quantity Ordered measure displays the quantity values with the unit of measure.

Create a CompositeProvider
for the Consolidated Open ODS view

To utilize the navigation attributes of the Orders data model, we will create
a final CompositeProvider object on top of the Orders ALL (ZINTFCT01)
Open ODS View object. Figure 6-42 presents the structure of the Orders
(ZCPINTFCT01) CompositeProvider object.

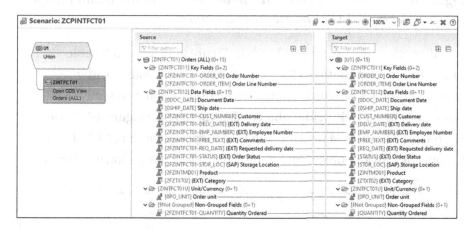

Figure 6-42. *Defining the structure of the ZCPINTFCT01
CompositeProvider object*

The ZCPINTFCT01 CompositeProvider object sources data from the
Orders (ALL) Open ODS View object that was created in the previous
section. All the fields have been mapped from the source into the target.
To show the available navigation attributes, in the *Source* section right-
click the Open ODS View icon and select *Show Unassigned Navigation
Attributes* (Figure 6-43).

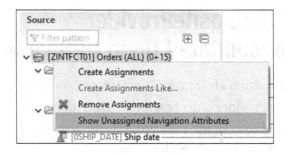

Figure 6-43. *Show Unassigned Navigation Attributes menu item for the ZCPINTFCT01 CompositeProvider object*

After selecting the option shown in Figure 6-43, we will be able to add Product attributes to the output of the CompositeProvider object. Optionally we could enable navigation attributes directly from the CompositeProvider object's Output tab (see Figure 4-23 as a reference). Figure 6-44 presents the final mapping for the ZCPINTFCT01 CompositeProvider object including the Product navigation attributes.

![Source and Target mapping structure of the ZCPINTFCT01 CompositeProvider object]

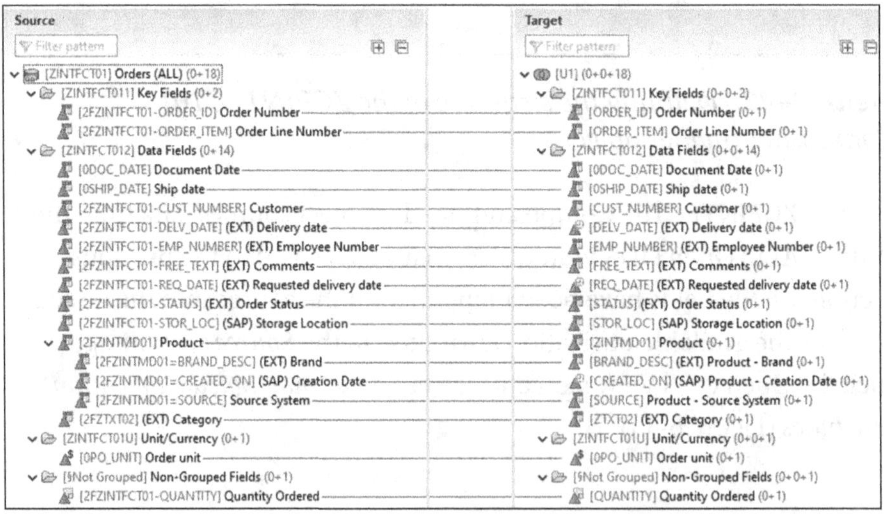

Figure 6-44. *Final structure of the ZCPINTFCT01 CompositeProvider object*

Figure 6-44 presents the target mapping for the ZCPINTFCT01
CompositeProvider object. For the navigation attribute descriptions, it is good
to include the information about the source object from which the column
was retrieved. This is why the description for the Product navigation attributes
were adjusted; i.e., (EXT) Brand was changed to (EXT) Product – Brand. This
will help the end user to identify that this information comes from the master
data of the Product dimension and not from transactional data. After activating
the CompositeProvider object, we can create the final query (Figure 6-45).

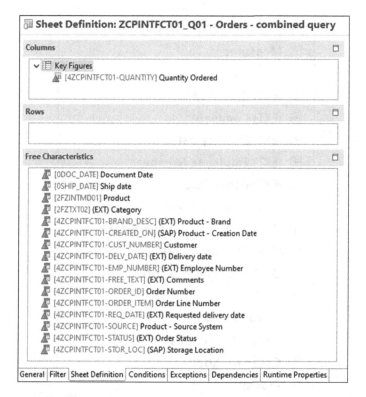

Figure 6-45. *Definition of the ZCPINTFCT01_Q01 query*

In the final query, we defined the target structure of the report. The
Quantity Ordered measure was added to the *Columns* section. All the
attributes were added to the *Free Characteristics section* (Figure 6-45). Finally,
to validate the report, we will open it in the Analysis for Microsoft Excel tool.

First, when we open the report, we can see that thanks to the prefixes that we added for the descriptions, the fields are sorted (Figure 6-46). The end user can easily identify fields that are relevant for one or another data source. The fields that are common for both sources are shown at the bottom of the list without prefixes. To validate the content of the report, we can add selected fields to the output of the crosstab (Figure 6-47).

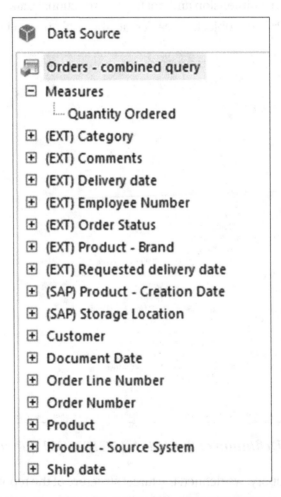

Figure 6-46. Display list of fields for the ZCPINTFCT01_Q01 query in Analysis for Microsoft Excel

Order Number	Order Line Number	Document Date	Product	Product - Source System	(EXT) Product - Brand	(SAP) Product - Creation Date	Quantity Ordered
0000000001	001	17.08.2004	A/C Gas Receiver	EXT	AUTOprism	#	25 EA
0000000001	002	17.08.2004	A/C Condenser Filter	EXT	AUTOprism	#	30 EA
4500000494	000010	21.12.2009	Coolant temperature sensor	SAP	#	01.03.2003	12 EA
4500000494	000020	21.12.2009	Coolant temperature sensor	SAP	#	01.03.2003	138 EA

Figure 6-47. *Output of the ZCPINTFCT01_Q01 query in Analysis for Microsoft Excel*

Figure 6-47 shows the output of the ZCPINTFCT01_Q01 for the selected fields. The fields that are relevant only for the specific data source contain the source system prefix in the header name. This informs us that for the given column the data will be available only for the specific system. If values are not available, there will be hash (#) symbol displayed. In addition, the Product - Source System column helps to identify or filter the Products from specific source system. This report enables us to perform a detailed analysis of all the orders across the company, no matter if they are coming from SAP or from the external system.

Summary

In this chapter, we showed how to combine SAP and non-SAP data into a single integrated star schema data model. We utilized the SAP HANA platform to build the virtual layer for combining both transactional and master datasets. After going through the scenario, you should also notice how big a role the good technical analysis plays, before implementing the actual solution.

Integrating multiple systems on the BW/4HANA platform can bring a lot of new insights to the business users and enable us to implement the global reporting solutions, while ensuring that the proper security model is maintained from the single system.

The new features and flexibility that were introduced with the latest release of the SAP BW/4HANA platform significantly simplify the integration of external data compared to the old legacy BW system.

APPENDIX A

Eclipse Installation

The Eclipse Modeling Tools software can be downloaded from the official Eclipse website:

```
https://www.eclipse.org/downloads/packages/
```

Once Eclipse is installed, you will also need to install Eclipse add-ons for the SAP Modeling Tools software. You can download and install the add-ons directly from Eclipse. Go to the SAP Development Tools site to check for the correct software version:

```
https://tools.hana.ondemand.com/
```

Copy the respective software site URL, select Help ➤ Install a new software from the Eclipse toolbar, and paste the URL in the "Work with" section. Then select the required tools and start the installation. Figure A-1 shows how to install SAP Development Tools for the Eclipse version 2020-03.

© Konrad Załęski 2021
K. Załęski, *Data Modeling with SAP BW/4HANA 2.0*,
https://doi.org/10.1007/978-1-4842-7089-9

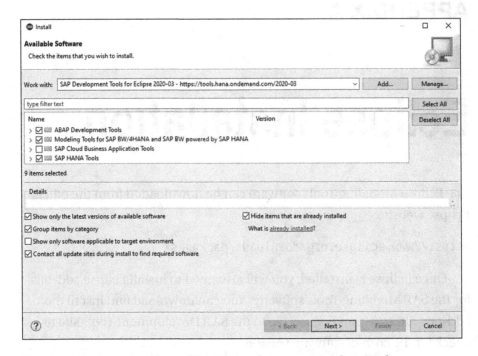

Figure A-1. *Installation of SAP Development Tools in Eclipse*

Note   Before you download the Eclipse software, check the SAP Development Tools site to see whether the SAP add-ons support a specific Eclipse version.

After completing the installation, you will be able to use the SAP modeling perspectives. To select the desired perspective, choose Window ➤ Perspective ➤ Open Perspective ➤ Other from the Eclipse toolbar. The perspective selection window will open, as in Figure A-2.

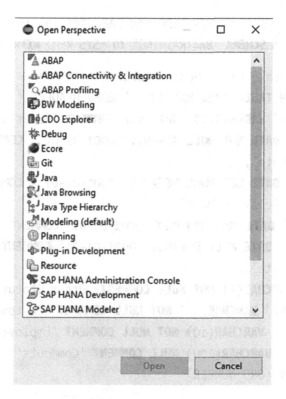

Figure A-2. *Eclipse modeling perspectives*

Once SAP Modeling Tools is installed, you can start using the Eclipse environment.

SQL Scripts

Here are the SQL scripts that you can use:

```
/********* Create new database schema *********/
CREATE SCHEMA "BW4TRAINING";
```

```
/*** Grant access to _SYS_REPO and SAP user for the schema ***/
GRANT SELECT ON SCHEMA "BW4TRAINING" TO _SYS_REPO WITH GRANT OPTION;

/********* Create Order Header table *********/
CREATE COLUMN TABLE "BW4TRAINING"."ORDER_HEADER" (
  "ORD_NUMBER" VARCHAR(10) NOT NULL COMMENT 'Order Number',
  "DOC_DATE" DATE NOT NULL DEFAULT '0001-01-01'  COMMENT
  'Document Date',
  "REQ_DATE" DATE NOT NULL DEFAULT '0001-01-01'  COMMENT
  'Requested Delivery Date',
  "SHIP_DATE" DATE NULL DEFAULT '0001-01-01' COMMENT 'Ship Date',
  "DELV_DATE" DATE NULL DEFAULT '0001-01-01' COMMENT
  'Delivery Date',
  "STATUS" VARCHAR(3) NOT NULL COMMENT 'Order Status',
  "CUST_NUMBER" VARCHAR(10) NOT NULL COMMENT 'Customer Number',
  "EMP_NUMBER" VARCHAR(10) NOT NULL COMMENT 'Employee Number',
  "FREE_TEXT" VARCHAR(100) NULL COMMENT 'Comments',
  PRIMARY KEY (ORD_NUMBER)
);

/********* Create Order Details table *********/
CREATE COLUMN TABLE "BW4TRAINING"."ORDER_DETAILS" (
  "ORD_NUMBER" VARCHAR(10) NOT NULL COMMENT 'Order Number',
  "ORD_ITEM" VARCHAR(3) NOT NULL COMMENT 'Order Line Number',
  "PRODUCT_ID"  VARCHAR(10) NOT NULL COMMENT 'Product ID',
  "CATEGORY_ID" VARCHAR(5) NOT NULL COMMENT 'Category ID',
  "QTY" INT NOT NULL COMMENT 'Quantity Ordered',
  PRIMARY KEY ("ORD_NUMBER","ORD_ITEM")
);
```

```
/********* Create Order Status table *********/
CREATE COLUMN TABLE "BW4TRAINING"."ORDER_STATUS" (
  "STATUS_ID" VARCHAR(3) NOT NULL COMMENT 'Status ID',
  "STATUS_DESC" VARCHAR(30) NOT NULL COMMENT 'Status Name',
  "LANGU" VARCHAR(2) NOT NULL COMMENT 'Language',
  PRIMARY KEY ("STATUS_ID","LANGU")
);

/********* Create Products table *********/
CREATE COLUMN TABLE "BW4TRAINING"."PRODUCTS" (
  "PRODUCT_ID"  VARCHAR(10) NOT NULL COMMENT 'Product ID',
  "CATEGORY_ID" VARCHAR(5) NOT NULL COMMENT 'Category ID',
  "PRODUCT_DESC" VARCHAR(200) NULL COMMENT 'Description',
  "BRAND_DESC" VARCHAR(200) NULL COMMENT 'Brand',
  "PRICE" DECIMAL(10,2) NOT NULL COMMENT 'Price',
  "CURRENCY" VARCHAR(3) NOT NULL COMMENT 'Currency',
  PRIMARY KEY ("PRODUCT_ID","CATEGORY_ID")
);

/********* Create Product Categories table *********/
CREATE COLUMN TABLE "BW4TRAINING"."CATEGORIES" (
  "CATEGORY_ID" VARCHAR(5) NOT NULL COMMENT 'Category ID',
  "CATEGORY_DESC" VARCHAR(200) NULL COMMENT 'Description',
  PRIMARY KEY ("CATEGORY_ID")
);

/********* Populate Order Header data *********/
INSERT INTO "BW4TRAINING"."ORDER_HEADER" VALUES (
'0000000001','2004-08-17','2004-08-27','2004-08-19',ADD_
DAYS('2004-08-19',7),'001','0100000010','0300000001',NULL);
INSERT INTO "BW4TRAINING"."ORDER_HEADER" VALUES (
'0000000002','2004-08-19','2004-08-28','2004-08-23',ADD_
DAYS('2004-08-23',8),'001','0100000011','0300000001',NULL);
```

```
INSERT INTO "BW4TRAINING"."ORDER_HEADER" VALUES (
'0000000003','2004-08-20','2004-08-26','2004-08-22',ADD_
DAYS('2004-08-22',9),'001','0100000011','0300000001',NULL);
INSERT INTO "BW4TRAINING"."ORDER_HEADER" VALUES (
'0000000004','2004-08-20','2004-08-30','2004-08-23',ADD_
DAYS('2004-08-23',8),'001','0100000013','0300000001',NULL);
INSERT INTO "BW4TRAINING"."ORDER_HEADER" VALUES (
'0000000005','2004-08-21','2004-08-29','2004-08-26',ADD_
DAYS('2004-08-26',8),'001','0100000013','0300000001',NULL);
INSERT INTO "BW4TRAINING"."ORDER_HEADER" VALUES (
'0000000006','2004-08-27','2004-09-04','2004-08-31',ADD_
DAYS('2004-08-31',5),'001','0100000013','0300000001',NULL);
INSERT INTO "BW4TRAINING"."ORDER_HEADER" VALUES (
'0000000007','2004-08-28','2004-09-06','2004-09-01',ADD_
DAYS('2004-09-01',7),'001','0100000010','0300000001',NULL);
INSERT INTO "BW4TRAINING"."ORDER_HEADER" VALUES (
'0000000008','2004-08-30','2004-09-06','2004-09-01',ADD_
DAYS('2004-09-01',7),'001','0100000013','0300000002',NULL);
INSERT INTO "BW4TRAINING"."ORDER_HEADER" VALUES (
'0000000009','2004-09-01','2004-09-11','2004-09-05',ADD_
DAYS('2004-09-05',9),'001','0100000013','0300000002',NULL);
INSERT INTO "BW4TRAINING"."ORDER_HEADER" VALUES (
'0000000010','2004-09-03','2004-09-13','2004-09-04',ADD_
DAYS('2004-09-04',7),'001','0100000013','0300000002',NULL);
INSERT INTO "BW4TRAINING"."ORDER_HEADER" VALUES (
'0000000011','2004-09-07','2004-09-15','2004-09-13',ADD_
DAYS('2004-09-13',7),'001','0100000014','0300000002',NULL);
INSERT INTO "BW4TRAINING"."ORDER_HEADER" VALUES (
'0000000012','2004-09-08','2004-09-17','2004-09-14',ADD_
DAYS('2004-09-14',8),'001','0100000015','0300000002',NULL);
```

```
INSERT INTO "BW4TRAINING"."ORDER_HEADER" VALUES (
'0000000013','2004-09-08','2004-09-18','2004-09-11',ADD_
DAYS('2004-09-11',10),'001','0100000014','0300000002',NULL);
INSERT INTO "BW4TRAINING"."ORDER_HEADER" VALUES (
'0000000014','2004-09-09','2004-09-18',NULL,NULL,'002',
'0100000014','0300000002',NULL);
INSERT INTO "BW4TRAINING"."ORDER_HEADER" VALUES (
'0000000015','2004-09-10','2004-09-17',NULL,NULL,'002',
'0100000010','0300000002','Customer requested special shippment.');
INSERT INTO "BW4TRAINING"."ORDER_HEADER" VALUES (
'0000000016','2004-09-10','2004-09-17',NULL,NULL,'002',
'0100000010','0300000003',NULL);
INSERT INTO "BW4TRAINING"."ORDER_HEADER" VALUES (
'0000000017','2004-09-15','2004-09-22',NULL,NULL,'002',
'0100000011','0300000003',NULL);
INSERT INTO "BW4TRAINING"."ORDER_HEADER" VALUES (
'0000000018','2004-09-16','2004-09-22',NULL,NULL,'002',
'0100000011','0300000003',NULL);
INSERT INTO "BW4TRAINING"."ORDER_HEADER" VALUES (
'0000000019','2004-09-27','2004-10-05',NULL,NULL,'002',
'0100000011','0300000003',NULL);
INSERT INTO "BW4TRAINING"."ORDER_HEADER" VALUES (
'0000000020','2004-09-30','2004-10-10',NULL,NULL,'003',
'0100000014','0300000003','Customer credit limit exceeded.
Will ship when a payment is received.');

/********* Populate Order Details data *********/
INSERT INTO "BW4TRAINING"."ORDER_DETAILS" VALUES ('0000000001',
'001','AC001','0001',25);
INSERT INTO "BW4TRAINING"."ORDER_DETAILS" VALUES ('0000000001',
'002','AC002','0001',30);
```

```sql
INSERT INTO "BW4TRAINING"."ORDER_DETAILS" VALUES ('0000000002',
'001','AV004','0002',13);
INSERT INTO "BW4TRAINING"."ORDER_DETAILS" VALUES ('0000000002',
'002','CS002','0003',2);
INSERT INTO "BW4TRAINING"."ORDER_DETAILS" VALUES ('0000000002',
'003','CS006','0003',19);
INSERT INTO "BW4TRAINING"."ORDER_DETAILS" VALUES ('0000000003',
'001','AV003','0002',25);
INSERT INTO "BW4TRAINING"."ORDER_DETAILS" VALUES ('0000000004',
'001','AV004','0002',30);
INSERT INTO "BW4TRAINING"."ORDER_DETAILS" VALUES ('0000000005',
'001','AV004','0002',6);
INSERT INTO "BW4TRAINING"."ORDER_DETAILS" VALUES ('0000000006',
'001','CS005','0003',14);
INSERT INTO "BW4TRAINING"."ORDER_DETAILS" VALUES ('0000000006',
'002','AC003','0001',18);
INSERT INTO "BW4TRAINING"."ORDER_DETAILS" VALUES ('0000000006',
'003','AV001','0002',21);
INSERT INTO "BW4TRAINING"."ORDER_DETAILS" VALUES ('0000000006',
'004','AV004','0002',35);
INSERT INTO "BW4TRAINING"."ORDER_DETAILS" VALUES ('0000000006',
'005','CS002','0003',7);
INSERT INTO "BW4TRAINING"."ORDER_DETAILS" VALUES ('0000000006',
'006','CS006','0003',23);
INSERT INTO "BW4TRAINING"."ORDER_DETAILS" VALUES ('0000000007',
'001','CS003','0003',1);
INSERT INTO "BW4TRAINING"."ORDER_DETAILS" VALUES ('0000000008',
'001','CS003','0003',2);
INSERT INTO "BW4TRAINING"."ORDER_DETAILS" VALUES ('0000000009',
'001','CS003','0003',5);
```

```
INSERT INTO "BW4TRAINING"."ORDER_DETAILS" VALUES ('0000000010',
'001','CS003','0003',7);
INSERT INTO "BW4TRAINING"."ORDER_DETAILS" VALUES ('0000000011',
'001','AV001','0002',18);
INSERT INTO "BW4TRAINING"."ORDER_DETAILS" VALUES ('0000000012',
'001','AV001','0002',20);
INSERT INTO "BW4TRAINING"."ORDER_DETAILS" VALUES ('0000000013',
'001','AV001','0002',11);
INSERT INTO "BW4TRAINING"."ORDER_DETAILS" VALUES ('0000000014',
'001','CS003','0003',1);
INSERT INTO "BW4TRAINING"."ORDER_DETAILS" VALUES ('0000000015',
'001','AC001','0001',28);
INSERT INTO "BW4TRAINING"."ORDER_DETAILS" VALUES ('0000000015',
'002','AC002','0001',7);
INSERT INTO "BW4TRAINING"."ORDER_DETAILS" VALUES ('0000000015',
'003','AC003','0001',8);
INSERT INTO "BW4TRAINING"."ORDER_DETAILS" VALUES ('0000000016',
'001','AC002','0001',10);
INSERT INTO "BW4TRAINING"."ORDER_DETAILS" VALUES ('0000000017',
'001','CS003','0003',17);
INSERT INTO "BW4TRAINING"."ORDER_DETAILS" VALUES ('0000000018',
'001','CS005','0003',23);
INSERT INTO "BW4TRAINING"."ORDER_DETAILS" VALUES ('0000000019',
'001','CS005','0003',29);
INSERT INTO "BW4TRAINING"."ORDER_DETAILS" VALUES ('0000000020',
'001','CS003','0003',7);

/********* Populate Order Statuses data *********/
INSERT INTO "BW4TRAINING"."ORDER_STATUS" VALUES ( '001',
'Delivered', 'E');
INSERT INTO "BW4TRAINING"."ORDER_STATUS" VALUES ( '002',
'In Process', 'E');
```

```
INSERT INTO "BW4TRAINING"."ORDER_STATUS" VALUES ( '003',
'Rejected', 'E' );
INSERT INTO "BW4TRAINING"."ORDER_STATUS" VALUES ( '001',
'Geliefert', 'D' );
INSERT INTO "BW4TRAINING"."ORDER_STATUS" VALUES ( '002',
'In Bearbeitung', 'D' );
INSERT INTO "BW4TRAINING"."ORDER_STATUS" VALUES ( '003',
'Abgelehnt', 'D' );

/********* Populate Products data *********/
INSERT INTO "BW4TRAINING"."PRODUCTS" VALUES
('AC001','0001','A/C Gas Receiver','AUTOprism',70,'USD');
INSERT INTO "BW4TRAINING"."PRODUCTS" VALUES
('AC002','0001','A/C Condenser Filter','AUTOprism',150,'USD');
INSERT INTO "BW4TRAINING"."PRODUCTS" VALUES
('AC003','0001','A/C Cabin Filter','AUTOprism',30,'USD');
INSERT INTO "BW4TRAINING"."PRODUCTS" VALUES
('AV001','0002','Radio and media player','Fly
Audio',120,'USD');
INSERT INTO "BW4TRAINING"."PRODUCTS" VALUES
('AV002','0002','Speaker','Fly Audio',60,'USD');
INSERT INTO "BW4TRAINING"."PRODUCTS" VALUES
('AV003','0002','Tuner','Fly Audio',80,'USD');
INSERT INTO "BW4TRAINING"."PRODUCTS" VALUES
('AV004','0002','Antenna ','Fly Audio',30,'USD');
INSERT INTO "BW4TRAINING"."PRODUCTS" VALUES
('CS001','0003','Arm Rest','Exclusive Car Interior',65,'USD');
INSERT INTO "BW4TRAINING"."PRODUCTS" VALUES
('CS002','0003','Bucket seat','Exclusive Car
Interior',465,'USD');
```

INSERT INTO "BW4TRAINING"."PRODUCTS" **VALUES**
('CS003','0003','Children and baby car seat','Exclusive Car
Interior',170,'USD');
INSERT INTO "BW4TRAINING"."PRODUCTS" **VALUES**
('CS005','0003','Seat belt','MotoSpec',30,'EUR');
INSERT INTO "BW4TRAINING"."PRODUCTS" **VALUES**
('CS006','0003','Seat bracket','MotoSpec',75,'EUR');

/********* Populate Categories data *********/
INSERT INTO "BW4TRAINING"."CATEGORIES" **VALUES** ('0001','Air
conditioning system (A/C)');
INSERT INTO "BW4TRAINING"."CATEGORIES" **VALUES** ('0002','Audio/
video devices');
INSERT INTO "BW4TRAINING"."CATEGORIES" **VALUES** ('0003','Car seat');

Index

© Konrad Załęski 2021
K. Załęski, *Data Modeling with SAP BW/4HANA 2.0*,
https://doi.org/10.1007/978-1-4842-7089-9

Printed in the United States
by Baker & Taylor Publisher Services